HOT SHOTS
OF PRO BASKETBALL

Action-packed profiles of pro basketball's super-scoring superstars. Included are some of the flashiest players in the NBA and ABA: Julius Erving, Pete Maravich, Artis Gilmore, Rick Barry, Walt Frazier, George McGinnis, Spencer Haywood, Geoff Petrie, and Kareem Abdul-Jabbar.

HOT SHOTS
OF PRO BASKETBALL
BY LOU SABIN

illustrated with photographs

Random House · New York

PHOTOGRAPH CREDITS: Vernon J. Biever, 37, 72, 83, 145; Clifton Boutelle, 97; Malcolm W. Emmons, 2–3, 7, 10, 15, 24, 32, 42, 51, 54, 70, 102, 104, 111, 120, 139, 142; Ronald C. Modra, 85; Darryl Norenberg (Camera 5), 56; Ken Regan (Camera 5), 66, 80; United Press International, endpapers, 19, 40, 63, 75, 90, 108, 115, 118, 125, 131; Wide World Photos, 22, 29, 47, 128, 132. Cover photo by Malcolm W. Emmons.

Copyright © 1974 by Random House, Inc.
All rights reserved under International and Pan-American Copyright Conventions. Published in the United States by Random House, Inc., New York, and simultaneously in Canada by Random House of Canada Limited, Toronto.

Library of Congress Cataloging in Publication Data
Sabin, Louis. Hot shots of pro basketball. (Pro basketball library)
SUMMARY: Profiles of nine professional basketball superstars with exceptional scoring records.
1. Basketball—Biography—Juvenile literature. [1. Basketball—Biography] I. Title.
GV884.A1S214 1974   796.32′3′0922[B][920]   74-4932
ISBN 0-394-82901-8   ISBN 0-394-92901-2 (lib. bdg.)

Manufactured in the United States of America   1 2 3 4 5 6 7 8 9 0

For my mother, for whom this sign of appreciation is long overdue.

Special thanks to Nick Curran and the NBA Public Relations staff and to the offices of the ABA, Indiana Pacers, and New York Nets.

Contents

Introduction	8
Julius Erving	11
Pete Maravich	25
Artis Gilmore	43
Rick Barry	57
Walt Frazier	73
George McGinnis	91

Spencer Haywood	105
Geoff Petrie	121
Kareem Abdul-Jabbar	133
Index	149

Introduction

Meet the "hot shots," that unique group of basketball players who can turn a crowd on while they turn a game around. They do it in many ways, but each one does his thing with a special style that, once seen, is never forgotten.

Most of these superstars catch the fancy of the fans with their shooting—the awesome slam-dunk that can shatter a backboard or bend a hoop out of shape; the net-rippling jumper that follows a series of spinning, twisting moves; the floating two-pointer at the end of a long, swooping flight from the foul line, or a wild three-pointer from wa-a-ay out.

Some earn the hot-shot label with ball handling —the dazzling dribble through the legs, hand-to-hand, shifting direction; the blurringly swift behind-the-back pass, or the on-the-mark blind feed to an open man. Still others captivate the crowd with their almost superhuman defense—the split-second reflexes and darting hands that rack up steal after steal; the strength and determination that intimidate opposing shooters. And there are some that become hot shots without even trying—there's just something about them that catches the attention of the fans and the press.

The men in the spotlight are not always applauded, however. While most fans thrill to the hot shots' razzle-dazzle moves, others accuse them of being "showboats" or "ball hogs." But love 'em or hate 'em, you can't ignore them! Their actions attract millions of fans who follow them closely and cheer or boo them with special glee. Adding a rare dimension to an already exciting sport, they make basketball more than just a game played for victories, money, and fame. They make it an art.

So here are nine of basketball's brightest stars—the hot shots.

Julius Erving

"I have a wild imagination," Julius Erving once said. And no one who ever saw the incredible Dr. J. operate could doubt that statement. The high-flying super-scoring hot shot had a thousand basketball moves—and no two, it seemed, were alike.

Playing for the Virginia Squires in 1973, he unveiled a new move that left even the most ardent Erving admirers gasping. In a game against the San Diego Conquistadors, Erving pulled down a defensive rebound and leaped high in the air to pass it off to the Squires' open man—just as a big Conquistador moved right into his path. Suspended in the air, Julius realized that his intended pass would surely be blocked. Time seemed to stop as he hung there in space. Then, still airborne, he whirled around in a full 360-degree circle, switched the ball to his left hand, and tossed it to teammate Bernie Williams, who dropped in the easy lay-up.

After the game, San Diego assistant coach Stan Albeck told Erving, "Man, I thought I'd seen everything. But that 360-degree job—nobody's ever done anything like that. It was unbelievable."

But, of course, Julius Erving had been doing the unbelievable for years—first in a New York playground, then in a college gymnasium, and finally in a jam-packed pro arena.

Julius was born on February 22, 1950, in Hempstead, a town on Long Island, New York. "We were very poor," he said, recalling his childhood. "My parents separated when I was three. My mother did domestic work, cleaning other people's houses. We lived in a project and received social services. My mother raised us—my sister Alexis, my brother Marvin, and me. And I really appreciate what she was doing all those years. She put food on the table. When I asked her for sneakers that were better, she got them. We didn't ask her for much, but if we wanted it, she got it."

Mrs. Erving later remarried, and the family moved to nearby Roosevelt when Julius was 13. It was a shift from one poor neighborhood to another, but it was there that Julius discovered a possible way out of the world of poverty. He was a bright, intelligent boy, and he put that talent to work in school. He also loved sports, and he worked hard at that, too. School and non-basketball time were spent seriously and thoughtfully, but basketball time was something else.

"I used to watch games on TV," he said. "My palms would sweat, and I'd think of moves no one else had done. I'd learn by watching good guys and bad guys. I'd dream up fantastic moves and then go out on the court and make them work."

The court Julius usually played on was in Roosevelt Park. It was made of concrete, painted green with white lines, and had two baskets—a far cry from the polished, hardwood boards that would become the stage for his brilliant college and professional performances. But it was on that "playground schoolroom" that he learned his lessons in shooting and dribbling.

"If somebody else was around," he recalled, "I'd play one-on-one, a hundred points wins. We didn't play for money. We played for ego, for pride."

The one-on-one games gave him the chance to test the fantastic moves he practiced when he played alone. "Some of those moves took a long time to develop," he said.

The moves and shots paid off, again and again. First they made him the big man of the neighborhood playground. Soon his reputation spread, and he was challenged by the other top city schoolyard players. Julius answered each challenge with a staggering array of basketball weaponry, not the least of which were his dunks. On one play he might use the easy little hop up, from right under the basket, plopping the ball through the hoop. It looked simple, but to gain the position that made the shot itself seem like a snap, he first had to outmaneuver—and outwit—his rival. Then there were his more spectacular slam-dunks, the backboard-shaking reverse stuffs and the totally ego-crushing behind-the-head dumps he executed, grinning into the eyes of his opponent as the ball swished through the cords.

"There's a whole psychology there that makes you want to beat a guy in a way that makes him pay twice," Erving said of those playground days. "You want to outscore him, and you also want to freak him out with a big move or a big block. That way, even if the score is tied, you and he both know you're really ahead."

It was around that time that Julius Erving acquired the nickname of Dr. J., which stuck with him throughout his life. As he recalled it, "When we were in Roosevelt, we would fool around and talk about being philosophers and doctors when we grew up. I was gonna be a doctor."

He was also going to be tall when he grew up, but he didn't know that then. "I was always small," he later said, thinking back to the days before he reached his full height and weight of 6-foot-7 and

Julius Erving: the incredible Doctor J.

200 pounds. "I was only 6-foot-3 when I graduated from high school. Yet I always had big hands and could jump, so I learned to be trickier than the bigger guys. I liked to experiment.

"I was a good, but not great, high school basketball player until my junior year. Scholastically, I was ahead of my physical self. In my junior year I gave up all other sports and played only basketball because I really dug it and saw it as a means to an end—going to college."

The college he chose, from among more than 100 offers, was the University of Massachusetts. He picked it over such better-known schools as St. John's and Penn State "because it wasn't a meat-grinder school, where they just use your body. The UMass coach, Jack Lehman, was concerned about *me*."

Dr. J. was an instant sensation at the University of Massachusetts, where he tore into the competition in his first varsity year. The super-sophomore wrapped up the season with averages of 26 points and 20 rebounds a game. In his junior year he gave a repeat performance. He averaged 27 points a game and led the nation's college stars in the rebounding category with a per-game average of 19. As good as they were, those statistics, recorded against such weak competition as Bates, Colby, and Amherst, weren't impressive enough to win many votes from the people who pick All-America teams. But Julius more than impressed the ABA's Virginia Squires, who knew a great player when they saw one.

Although the Doctor wanted to finish college, the Squires' offer of a four-year, $500,000 contract was too strong a lure to resist. So Erving left UMass before the start of his senior year to launch his legendary career in professional basketball.

From the opening game of his first pro season, Dr. J. was as electrifying as a bolt of lightning. The young rookie finished the 1971–72 season sixth in scoring, with a per-game mark of 27.3, and his 15.7 rebounds snared third place in the league's carom competition. After racking up 20 points in the All-Star game, he went on to top everybody in championship playoff scoring with an average of 33.3 points a contest.

Erving was edged out of the ABA's Rookie of the Year award for 1972 by a 7-foot-2 giant named Artis Gilmore. But if Dr. J. didn't get the award, he certainly got the raves. "With a little more experience," predicted Squires coach Al Bianchi, "he'll be the best forward who ever played the game. Absolutely the best. The only one who compares to Julie is Elgin Baylor [whose marvelous NBA career ended with the 1971–72 season]. They both have great body control. Julie can put the ball down just as well as Baylor, he can shoot as well, he can rebound better, run better, play defense a heck of a lot better, and Julie can shoot with both hands."

Because that opinion came from Erving's own coach, some people might have considered it a prejudiced point of view. But there was no reason to doubt the words of a rival forward, Kentucky's All-Star Dan Issel, who declared, "There's nobody in pro basketball who compares with Julius Erving, let alone in the ABA. He's so smooth, and everything seems to come so easy to him. I'm sure he works at his game, but it all seems so effortless."

Then Issel added wistfully, "There are a lot of things he does I wish I could do, and I don't think there's anything I can do that he wishes he could do."

In fact, it often seemed as if there was *nothing* Dr. J. couldn't do. He'd come roaring downcourt, the ABA ball looking as small as a red-white-and-blue balloon in his huge hands. Then he would pass off to a teammate, put some moves on the man guarding him, and glide gracefully toward the foul line. A moment later someone would hit him with a pass. He'd pluck it out of the air in mid-stride and take off like an eagle, his long arms outstretched. And before his sneakers slapped against the floor, the ball would be slamming through the net. Score two more for the high-flying forward who brought his own trapeze act to basketball.

"He comes at you with those long, open strides," said Doug Moe, a guard who often fed those passes to Julius when they played together for the Squires, "and you have a tendency to keep backing away from him because you think he's not really into his move yet. If you keep backing, if you fail to go up and challenge him, he'll simply glide right by you."

Dunking, swooping by for drop-in buckets, twisting and shoving home reverse lay-ups, popping in two- and three-pointers from 15 to 25 feet away, Erving made the 1972–73 season one to remember. He was named to the ABA All-Star

Head and shoulders above the crowd, Virginia's Julius Erving leaps for the rebound in a 1972 game against the New York Nets.

Team for the second year in a row, and continued to dazzle his fans on offense and defense. The good Doctor's 12.2 rebounds a game were sixth best in the league, just a fraction below the men who finished fifth, fourth, and third. His 181 steals made the fast-handed forward the third highest ball thief in the ABA. And when it came to scoring, Dr. J. was truly number one. His 32 points a game average put him a full three-and-a-half points ahead of runner-up George McGinnis.

But it was the quality—not the quantity—of his shots that made Erving so spectacular. As the Squires' Neal Johnson put it, "Last year he used to blow my mind with a new move about three times a game. Now it's *only* about once a game that he'll do something that will leave the guys on the bench looking at each other and just sort of shaking their heads. He's too much!"

Unfortunately, the Squires were having financial problems and felt that Julius' salary demands were also too much. Erving wasn't satisfied with his contract arrangements, and he and the Squires management were unable to reach an agreement. Everybody concerned was growing unhappier by the day, until the New York Nets stepped in and solved the problem by making a trade with Virginia that pleased everyone—especially Dr. J. The move meant more than just a fatter paycheck, however. It also gave him a chance to do his fantastic act in the

Net arena, located just a few miles away from his hometown on Long Island.

Dr. J. earned his higher salary right from the start. In addition to bringing thousands of new fans flocking to Net games in the 1973–74 season, he boosted the New Yorkers from their fourth place 1972–73 ranking to the top of the Eastern Division. Burning the baskets with more than 27 points a game, rebounding and playmaking, he did it all.

Net coach Kevin Loughery couldn't have been happier with the man who wore number 32 on his red-white-and-blue uniform. When the coach felt the Nets needed Julius' strength under the boards, the Doctor cured the team's rebounding ills; when Loughery turned to him for ball-hawking and blocking and tight guarding, the Doctor operated exactly the way a defensive specialist should. Even when Loughery asked him to sacrifice some of his point-making for the sake of team balance, Dr. J. agreed without a complaint. (At the time, Julius was battling McGinnis for the league scoring crown, and could hardly be blamed for wanting every basket he could get.) And, of course, when there was a need for a lot of points in a hurry, plus some dynamic play to inspire the rest of the team, the Doctor dug into his bag of tricks and concocted another magic potion.

"How can I be amazed at Dr. J. so often?" Loughery said in the middle of the 1973–74 cham-

Playing for the Nets in 1973, Dr. J. puts one of his fantastic moves on Kentucky's Artis Gilmore.

pionship race. "Because he does things no one else in this game can do, and it's something different every time. I've never seen anybody like him."

Doing everything that was asked of him, Julius still captured the scoring championship, his 27.3 points-per-game average far outdistancing runner-up George McGinnis' 25.8. Erving was also sixth in the league's assists department, seventh in rebounding, and third in blocked shots and steals. He really did it all and was suitably rewarded with the ABA's Most Valuable Player award.

And with Doctor J. leading them, the New York Nets also did it all—going all the way to their first ABA championship. As Loughery said, echoing the opinions of thousands of Julius Erving fans all over the country, "There's never been anybody else like him." And there probably never will be.

Pete Maravich

Of all the "hot shots" in professional basketball, no one enjoyed the spotlight more than Peter Press Maravich. From grade school all the way to the NBA, Maravich the Magician wowed the crowds with a round-ball act that wouldn't have been out of place in a circus. He could do everything with a basketball, and everything he did left his fans begging for more—which was just the way Pete liked it.

"I guess there are several tons of ham in me," he admitted. "That must be obvious. And I recognized early that basketball, more than any other team game, gives a guy the opportunity to be a showman. The skills involved in basketball are different. You can do more stuff, more antics. And one guy has much more leeway to put on a show. That really is what basketball is for me—an entertainment, a chance to express myself. It's what I've chosen to do in my life; it's my thing."

Pete Maravich had been doing his thing for most of his young life. The Pistol Pete Show got underway in Sewickley, Pennsylvania, on June 22, 1948. In many ways, Pete seemed born to play basketball. His father, Press, was a fine player himself and had been a guard with the American Basketball League's Pittsburgh Ironmen and Youngstown Bears. One of the first presents he gave little Pete was a basketball. Pete's mother remembered that the little blond-haired boy "carried a basketball while other kids carried teddy bears."

Press gave Pete as much encouragement to play as is humanly possible. From the beginning, the elder Maravich gave his son a complete basketball education—talking it, playing it, and watching it day in, day out, year after year. And Pete was an able—and willing—pupil.

As he told a reporter many years later, "I guess I love the game of basketball more than anything else in the world. From the beginning it was like an addiction with me, I played it so much. Forty-seven weeks out of the year. Four to five hours a day. I never really was interested in other sports or anything else, either. For a while I ran some track. But I could never see running around in a circle for a long time and just getting tired. Really, it was all basketball. The fact that my father was coaching the game probably had the most to do with it. I mean, if he had put a football in my hand, I would have wanted to be a football player."

Press, who entered the ranks of coaching when his playing days ended, kept feeding the ball to Pete with the regularity of a machine. A typical scene would open with Pete coming home from school to find his father waiting. Did Press say anything about homework? Well, homework could always be done after dinner, when there was no longer enough light to practice on the court in the backyard. "I'd see Pete coming in the yard," Press said, "and I'd run for the basketball and start shooting. Wherever we lived, I always had a basket in the backyard."

A ball, a boy, and his father. It was basketball talk at dinner, and on rainy days. And it was run-and-shoot in the backyard, at the local YMCA, at the grade-school gymnasium. A similar routine continued as Pete moved to Daniel High School in Clemson, North Carolina; Needham-Broughton High in Raleigh, North Carolina; and Edwards Military Academy in Salemburg, North Carolina.

At school, at home—everywhere—a basketball was as much a part of young Pete as his right arm. Not only did he practice dribbling as he walked along the country roads, he even took the ball with him to the local movie house. He would sit in an aisle seat at the theater and dribble the ball on the carpeted floor while watching the picture. The other viewers may have wondered about the rhythmical thump-thump-thump coming from somewhere in the darkness, but apparently no one ever complained.

Pete made the starting line-up as an eighth-grader at Daniel High, and even then he was miles ahead of his older, taller teammates. But his first truly outstanding moment of scoring glory occurred in a game played for Edwards Military Academy. Pete recalled it this way: "One day I scored 50 points, and the next day the newspapers had it in big headlines. They just didn't seem to think it was possible for a prep-school kid to score that much in one game. I think that kicked everything off. After that, folks got to be conscious of how many points I scored from game to game."

And so the Pete Maravich legend began. Pete was named to the Prep School All-America team, and an avalanche of scholarship offers poured in from all over the country. Some colleges figured that the best way to get Pete to enroll was to recruit his father as the coach. One of those schools was Louisiana State University, and it was there that Pete and Press finally decided to go. LSU had been a basketball power in the early 1950s when the fabulous Bob Pettit starred there. But since then,

As a college player at Louisiana State University, Pete Maravich talks things over with his father—and coach—Press Maravich.

basketball had taken a back seat to the school's football teams.

"I always wanted to play for my dad," Pete said, "and I think, too, that he secretly wanted to coach me. We both knew how difficult it would be if we went to the same school, but the chance to revive basketball at a place like LSU was a challenge."

What Pete brought to LSU was an immense talent for scoring and passing. And, of course, he also brought his bag of crowd-thrilling tricks. Pete called it Show Time. All those years of practicing tricky moves, artful dribbling, and razzle-dazzle scoring had made him a one-of-a-kind player—and the nation's number one young hot shot.

Long before he came to LSU, Pete and his fans had formed a mutual admiration society. Pete proudly recreated one memorable pre-college game when the audience seemed especially appreciative. "It was a high school contest," he recalled, "and I began throwing wilder passes and connecting with them. The crowds were getting bigger then, and once I had the people behind me, I wanted to do more and more with the ball. I remember I threw a behind-the-back bounce pass on the move through a guy's legs! Oh, whoa!

"I was coming down on a three-on-one break, and my man was overplaying me to the left and giving me the open teammate on the right. But that was too easy a pass. We were going to get two points anyway, so it didn't make any difference. As my man was sliding and I was dribbling, I noticed his legs moving in and out. Still on the move, I saw the right moment and threw the ball when his legs were out—behind my back, now, not a straight pass—and I put it right through him to a teammate on the left. He converted it for the basket. The crowd, boy—the crowd, I want to tell you, went berserk. I couldn't believe it."

The people who came to watch Pete, the LSU freshman, could hardly believe him. By then he was known as Pistol Pete, a tribute to his being the "fastest shot in the country." Along with the nickname, he was also acquiring an image as a lovable, colorful clown. His floppy socks and wild-flying long hair only added to his attractiveness as a basketball personality.

The student body cheered and gasped in awe as their Pistol ran, shot, and passed the freshman squad to a 16–1 record. In those 17 games Maravich averaged a staggering 43.6 points per game and shot a solid 45 percent from the floor. Still, the Pistol had his doubters. Amid all the raves were some knocks at his ability to burn up the nets once he began playing varsity ball against some tougher competition. One critic predicted, "Maravich won't be so hot when he tries his fancy stuff on juniors and seniors, who have a lot more experience and class than the freshmen he fooled last year."

Pete's father, still his strongest booster, disagreed emphatically. "Pete's freshman year was just a preview," he said. "Wait'll you see him with the varsity. It'll be something extra special. As for his shooting so much, I'd have to be crazy not to let him shoot. He can do more things with the ball and

Socks and hair flopping, Pistol Pete decides what to do with the ball during a game at LSU.

without it than any other kid in the country. Cousy [the Boston Celtics' All-Star guard] never saw such moves. Will he be this team's leading scorer? You bet your life he will, unless he breaks both legs. And if I know him, even that won't stop him. This kid lives for basketball. He'll play, and he'll shoot just as often as he can get clear. No doubt about it."

As a sophomore in the 1967–68 season, Pete lived up to his father's expectations. In the opening game against the University of Tampa varsity, he was nothing less than great. He fired in 20 field goals and hit eight of nine foul shots for a sizzling total of 48 points. He also contributed 16 rebounds and four assists in the 97–81 rout of Tampa. And that was only the beginning.

In the next 17 games Pete scorched the nets, averaging more than 43 points a game. His single game high of 58 points tied the Southeastern Conference record set by LSU's last great hot shot, Bob Pettit, in the 1950s. Pete tied that mark in his seventh varsity game. Then he broke it in game number 21, against Alabama. Pete had 57 points with just seconds left to play. LSU's Tigers were ahead by eight points when teammate Ralph Jukkola recovered a loose ball. Instead of going back up with it for an easy two-pointer, he passed all the way out to mid-court, into the hands of a very surprised Pistol Pete.

"He yelled at me to shoot," Pete said afterward. "I didn't even know about the record, but apparently the other guys did. So I stepped toward the basket and let loose a silly two-handed push shot. Then I watched it go in."

That was one new mark with the name of Pete Maravich stamped on it, and by season's end there was still another. Pete's average of 43.8 points a game shattered the NCAA high of 41.7, set by Furman's Frank Selvy in 1953.

In his junior year (1968–69) Pete shot holes in his own year-old mark. Gunning home 1,148 points in 26 contests, he finished the season with an average of 44.2 points a game. But the Pistol wasn't finished yet. Still to come was his senior season, and he began it with his sharpshooter's eyes focused on two more records. One was his own brand-new season-average mark, which he wanted to raise even more. The other was Oscar Robertson's three-year scoring total of 2,973 points. "I've got 2,286," Pete said before the schedule began, "and if I stay healthy, maybe I can go after Oscar late in the season."

There were no "ifs" about it. Pete's senior year couldn't have been better. He wrapped up his college career by posting a 44.5 ppg average, again outdistancing his "old" record. He also blazed past The Big O's three-year total of 2,973 points with an accumulation of 3,667. As one sportswriter wrote,

"The nation hails Pete Maravich of Louisiana State University, college basketball's first point-a-minute scorer. Now it's on to the pros for Maravich the Magnificent. No matter which team he plays for, it has to be an improvement over his LSU running mates. Now he'll be among other talented men, who should help bring out the best of his shooting and passing skills."

And now he would, for the first time in his life, be out of the shadow and influence of his father. Pete signed a contract for almost two million dollars with the Atlanta Hawks, but this time Press Maravich was not part of the deal. The Hawks' coach was Richie Guerin and they weren't about to give him up.

However, even without Press's presence, Pete represented a major problem to Guerin. The Hawks had a strong team ready for the 1970–71 NBA season. The starting five of guards Lou Hudson and Walt Hazzard, forwards Joe Caldwell and Bill Bridges, and center Walt Bellamy was set. Yet Guerin knew the public would demand to see Pete in action—a lot and right away. He also knew that the players would resent having a rookie slipped into a potential championship line-up.

As one Hawk explained the team's dissatisfaction, "All of the starters are black, and we know that Atlanta's a Southern city that wants to see a white player break into the line-up. But it wouldn't be fair to us, especially when we have a shot at the title."

Guerin was caught between his team's feelings and the demands of the ticket-buying public, but his decision was a purely professional one. "The five best players will start," he declared. "I don't care who they are or what color they are or where they come from. If they can help this team, they'll play. We know Pete has great talent. We also know that he is a rookie and that he has much to learn about the pro game. If he proves good enough to handle it, he'll play. Until he does learn enough, he'll sit. Period."

The much-publicized rookie found the early going pretty rough. His moves were as sparkling as ever, and so was his pinpoint passing. But his solo style simply didn't fit into the professional style of team play.

For one thing, Pete wasn't taking percentage shots. Instead, he was firing whenever and wherever he felt the urge to fling the ball at the basket. He also wasn't working with his teammates on the play patterns that had been gone over and over in practice. He often passed when players weren't expecting the pass. He failed to play the kind of defense required at the top level of the sport. And time and again he was outmaneuvered or outwitted by rival guards who weren't about to be faked out by his fancy ball-handling and body-twisting.

Rookie Pete whizzes downcourt with the ball, pursued by Milwaukee veteran Oscar Robertson.

His freshman year was spent learning and adjusting to the big-league game. For long stretches of time, Pete found himself watching the action from the bench. "I know that my ball-handling can be much better than it's been," he admitted. "But these things are going to smooth themselves out. It's just like anything else where you're working with new people. It takes time to adjust to different players. For three seasons at LSU, I did nearly all the shooting, the dribbling, and the passing. I handled the ball 75 percent of the time. Not now, though. Now it's more like 90 percent of the time that I don't have the ball."

Pete did improve steadily as a rookie. And by season's end (which saw Atlanta make the playoffs but get eliminated in the first round) the Pistol had a 23.2 points-per-game scoring average. But although he had won the admiration of his Hawk teammates, he didn't come close to winning the Rookie of the Year award, which went to co-winners Dave Cowens and Geoff Petrie.

Pete was disappointed, and so was Coach Guerin. In Guerin's opinion, "Cowens and Petrie are fine players, but neither had a rookie year like Pete. And mark my words, neither will accomplish what Pete will accomplish in this league. I put him in the same class as Oscar Robertson, Jerry West, and Earl Monroe, when they came up. You know, it's difficult for a man Pete's age to handle the constant pressure that he was exposed to all year. He always impressed me the way he kept his cool through all the criticisms and hostilities that he had to face. To do all that and still have the rookie year he had, you gotta be some kind of ballplayer."

It was a wiser Pete Maravich who looked forward to the 1971–72 season. But a struggle with mononucleosis, which sapped his strength, kept him on the sidelines at the start of the year, and forced him to work long and hard to get back into shape. It was a rough campaign for him, and he received a large measure of credit from players, sportswriters, and fans for chalking up a 19.3 average for 66 games—and for sharpening his performance as a team player.

His health continued to plague Pete in the 1972–73 season. He suffered an attack of Bell's Palsy, which paralyzed part of his face for a portion of the year. But he overcame that, too, scoring at a handsome pace of 26.1 points a game, the fifth best average in the NBA. Pete also finished as the sixth highest assists man in the league, averaging 6.9 a game—an impressive total for someone who had often been accused of playing a one-man game.

In the 1973–74 season Pete's assists dropped, but his scoring increased to 27.7 points per game, good for second place in the NBA shooting race. Typical of the job Pete did in '73–74 was the game he turned in against the Houston Rockets. It started

Suspended in air, Maravich looks for a Hawk teammate during a 1973 game against the Kansas City–Omaha Kings.

off as a rare night for Maravich, whose shooting seemed to have cooled down several degrees. The Pistol fired one blank after another against the sturdy defense of Houston guard Mike Newlin. But suddenly, in the last three minutes of the game, Maravich came alive and gave the Hawks 15 straight points.

He didn't miss a shot in that splurge and all of them were difficult, from far outside and against rugged defense. The crowd roared as the final buzzer sounded—with the Hawks ahead 125–123. Even on a "cold" night, Maravich couldn't help being a hot shot when his team needed a little extra fire power.

That kind of wizardry made Pete the pet of Hawk fans, but the team's management was less impressed. They felt Pete was still playing too much of a one-man game and that his salary was too high for a team that wasn't making the post-season playoffs—or the money that goes with them. The result: in May 1974 Atlanta traded Maravich to the new NBA franchise in New Orleans, Louisiana.

The former LSU hot shot was glad to be going home to Louisiana—and, of course, the Louisiana fans were overjoyed to have their college scoring king back. So the Pistol packed his bag of tricks and headed further south, sure to be Dixieland's brightest shooting star.

Artis Gilmore

"Up, up, and awa-a-a-y!" Superman? No, it's the Kentucky Colonels' Supercenter, also known as Artis Gilmore. It was "up, up," as his highrise, 7-foot-2 body loomed over an opponent in midshot. And then, faster than a speeding bullet, it was "away," as one of Gilmore's huge hands slapped the basketball away from the basket.

Shot-blocking was the finest of Gilmore's many defensive weapons, and "stuffing a ball back down a shooter's throat" was an act he performed with ease and deep satisfaction. Gilmore didn't simply stop his opponents from scoring, he totally demoralized them. With the huge center ruling his "turf" around the key and backboard, opposing shooters often hesitated to even try a shot. As his Kentucky teammate, Dan Issel, said, "Artis's defense is just unbelievable. He can stop anybody."

Coming from Issel that was quite a compliment. Issel had been the Colonels' center until Gilmore's arrival moved him to a forward position, but he had nothing but praise for his replacement. "Artis makes life a lot easier for me now," said Issel. "I don't have to worry about the rebounding as much, and he's made us look a lot tougher on defense. I never saw Bill Russell in person, but I don't see how anyone can get as high as Gilmore."

Another pro, the ABA–NBA star Rick Barry, was equally enthusiastic about Gilmore's talents. Barry was playing with the New York Nets when Gilmore stormed the ABA as a rookie in 1971. "I played against Russell and Wilt Chamberlain and with Nate Thurmond," said Barry, "so I know how good they are. And this kid can be the same sort of dominating player. He has a natural knack for defense. I should know. He blocked five of my shots in one game."

Those comments came near the beginning of Gilmore's rookie year. Throughout that 1971–72 campaign, the young center continued to amaze his rivals and his teammates. He led the league in rebounding with 17.8 caroms a game and was tenth in scoring with an average of almost 24 points a game. His two-point field-goal shooting percentage was 59.8, another league-leading statistic. Harder to measure, but even more important, were the countless times he blocked shots and intimidated his foes.

Gilmore's outstanding freshman achievements led Bones McKinney, a former NBA star who was then vice-president of the Carolina Cougars, to say, "I'd pick him as the number one center in the ABA. Gilmore has improved more in a shorter time than any big man I've ever known. He has the ability now to go up in the air and decide whether he should or shouldn't try to block the shot—whether it will be a blocked shot or a goal-tending call against him. I don't know of a weakness he has except lack of experience. If I were starting a club today from scratch, I'd take him first."

Lack of experience is a problem that every rookie has to overcome, but in Gilmore's case it was even harder than usual. Unlike most youngsters who make it all the way to the pros, Gilmore was never a "basketball baby."

Born in Chipley, Florida, on September 21, 1949, Artis grew up poor. Of course, many other pros came from poor families, but they had playgrounds with real basketball courts and equipment. "When we were young," Gilmore said, "we didn't have the kind of things kids usually have growing up, like a basketball for Christmas. So we fixed up a bottomless peach basket and threw cans through it. We tried to follow the rules, and it was very entertaining because this was the best we could do."

Artis was the second of eight children, and the Gilmores had to do without more than just a basketball. "We went hungry sometimes," he recalled. "We went to school without shoes at times. I got so tired of eating fish my father caught that I don't want to look at another fish for a long time."

Despite the limited food, Artis had soared to a skinny 6-feet at the age of twelve. By the time he entered Chipley High School he had inched up to 6-foot-6. And by then he was using real basketballs instead of cans, and winning a name as a high school star. After playing three years in a Chipley uniform, he transferred to a school in nearby Dothan, Alabama, and finished his senior year with more excellent play.

Next came two years at Gardner-Webb Junior College, where his brilliant efforts caught the attention of more than 100 colleges. He chose Florida's Jacksonville University, a school that didn't have much of a basketball reputation, and became an immediate sensation. The Dolphins were soon winning more games and getting lots of newspaper, magazine, and television coverage, thanks to the devastating play of their do-it-all center.

Artis scored and rebounded in high double figures and racked up an impressive assists total. He contributed to the Dolphins' success in every

Even as a collegian at Jacksonville, Artis Gilmore (53) had a great ability to block shots. Here he stops a Western Kentucky shooter.

way possible, but the thing that really brought the fans up and screaming was his knack for blocking shots. "Going against Gilmore," moaned one weary rival center, "is like trying to outmaneuver a living derrick. You can't go around him, you can't go through him, and you sure as heck can't go over him."

Gilmore was just as steady and determined off the court. Although he hoped to move into the pro ranks, he wanted to get an education first. "I want a degree from college more than anything I can think of," he said. "My family has had it tough and I want to work with underprivileged kids in playgrounds and recreation centers. I had dreams of becoming a major-college basketball player, and it's a lot better than I expected. Now I want to help others get that opportunity."

Gilmore continued to shine throughout his college career. He was the NCAA's top man in rebounding and blocked shots, and he averaged 26.5 points on offense. He led the Dolphins all the way to the NCAA finals, and although Jacksonville was stopped short of the championship by a powerful UCLA team, no one could stop Gilmore. The Jacksonville Giant scored 132 points in five games and was voted to the All-Star Team.

Despite his fine record, however, many experts claimed that Gilmore was overrated and that his shooting wasn't up to pro standards. True, he was pouring in more than 26 points a game, but many of those baskets came on easy shots near the hoop. That was okay in college, said his critics, but he'd never get away with it in the pros.

A different evaluation of Gilmore's pro potential came from sportscaster Curt Gowdy, who wrote at the end of Artis's college career, "Towering Artis Gilmore had little opportunity to display his skills in tough competition before the NCAA last season. In fact, his credentials were suspect." Gowdy pointed out that Gilmore and the Dolphins had played against few really tough teams, but then he added, "Gilmore has developed a keen shooting eye (58 percent on field-goal attempts last season), but his true value is on defense, where he intimidates the opposition à la Bill Russell."

As a rookie with the Colonels, Gilmore's actions spoke louder than anyone's words. His super season earned him Rookie of the Year honors, the league's Most Valuable Player award, and a starting spot on the ABA's All-Star squad. In his second season (1972–73) Artis proved to be immune to the "sophomore slump." He averaged 20.8 points per game, won the rebound race, averaging 17.5 caroms per match, and set the pace in two-point field-goal percentage by hitting 56 percent of his shots. As for blocked shots, in the first year that statistics were kept on this important aspect of the sport, no other ABAer came close to his total of 259.

With Artis leading the way, Kentucky met the Indiana Pacers for the ABA championship. If there were any remaining doubts about Gilmore's place in the pros, his outstanding playoff performance had to erase them. In the third contest of the title series, the Kentucky Supercenter totally dominated the game. Artis—by this time nicknamed "The Intimidator" and "The Big One"—hooked and dunked for 28 points and banged the backboards for 16 rebounds. Even more exciting was his amazing defensive power.

Gilmore was officially credited with seven blocked shots, but, as one courtsider observed, "It seemed more like 18 blocks . . . or 40. Once he intimidated two Pacer shooters and blocked two shots, all on the same play. Once he came from near midcourt to bat loose a missed Colonel shot and saved the ball from going out of bounds, tossing it to Walt Simon at the same time as he was falling on the deck. And once in the fourth quarter he started at the free-throw line, took one gigantic step, and slammed home a dunk shot that sent bodies flying in three directions."

And in the end, when it got down to a two-point Kentucky lead and Indiana's George McGinnis drove full bore at the hoop, it was Artis Gilmore

Artis Gilmore: the Kentucky Colonels' supercenter.

who rose majestically above the pile-driving Pacer forward and flipped the shot away as if a fly was buzzing around his head.

Despite Gilmore's valiant efforts, the Pacers finally won the championship in the seventh and final game of the series. Although Artis didn't win a championship ring, he did win recognition as the league's premier center when he was voted to the 1973 All-League Team.

The assistant coach of the Colonels, Bud Olsen,

was especially delighted with Gilmore's progress. As a rookie, Artis had seemed reluctant to get his muscular-but-slender frame into the bruising give-and-take that has driven more than one promising player to the sidelines. But Olsen was teaching Gilmore how to hold his own against the toughest players in the ABA.

"Bud makes me work inside," said an appreciative Artis. "It's more the physical aspect than anything else. The same sort of stuff I get every time we play. He's right to do it. It's so different here than in college. Instead of meeting a top center every nine or ten games, in professional ball you get one about every night. You play the best competition, and the experience is bound to make you improve."

A two-time All-America in college, a super-everything as a pro rookie, the league's leading center every year—yet Artis always believed there was room for improvement. In an exhibition contest, which pitted him against Indiana's big center, Mel Daniels, Gilmore dumped in 33 points and snared 32 rebounds. Yet after the game Artis said, "I learned a lot from Daniels." And Daniels, still recovering from the drubbing Artis had given him, said, "I was interested to hear him say that. I'd like to know just what it was I taught him."

Throughout his career, Artis avoided making any comparisons between himself and the other great centers of basketball. "If there's a question that bothers me most," he once said, "it's 'Are you better than Bill Russell? Are you as good as Abdul-Jabbar? Are you in Wilt Chamberlain's category?' Once, a reporter told me he had seen a quote in which I claimed to be better than all three! Now, how do you answer those questions? It's impossible."

Gilmore answered the questions the only way an athlete can—by playing his game the best he could. A prime example was a game played midway through the 1973–74 season when the Colonels slaughtered the New York Nets, 123–91. A crucial factor in Kentucky's rout of the strong New York club was the ease with which Gilmore withstood the combined talents of Julius Erving, Billy Paultz, Willie Sojourner, Wendell Ladner, and Larry Kenon in the battle under the backboards. True to form, Gilmore contributed 21 points and picked up nine assists, and his shot-blocking—the official count of seven seemed low—was as fine as ever. It held down the Nets' scoring and also made them think twice before challenging the Jacksonville Giant standing guard between them and the basket. But what really stamped this game as a Gilmore Goodie was his supremacy in the rebound category.

Earlier in the season George McGinnis had set a new league rebound mark with 37. Artis may have

Gilmore shoots over New York's Billy Paultz in a 1974 game.

had that figure in mind as he fought for position at both ends of the court, swooped into the stratosphere, and clamped the ball in his vise-like grip. While the entire front line of the Nets combined for a total of 35 rebounds, Artis alone grabbed a grand total of 40.

It was a dazzling solo act that put an even glossier shine on Gilmore's already glowing star. Had there been a basketball equivalent of Hollywood's Academy Award for a single performance, The Big One would have won it right then and there.

Rick Barry

When Rick Barry made his first appearance on the NBA scene, his future as a professional looked as worthless as a canceled postage stamp. Just about everything he did in the early going of the 1965–66 season turned out wrong. Rick, a 6-foot-7½ All-America from the University of Miami, had won the NCAA scoring championship as a senior with a 37.4 points-per-game average. But now, a widely publicized rookie with the San Francisco Warriors, he was surrounded by other former All-Americas who made their living at this game. And one of the things they made a point of was putting super-rookies in their place.

In one of those early games, against the Baltimore Bullets, Rick found the going especially bumpy against a player named Ben Warley. Warley, a veteran of the basketball battlefields, was a little shorter and a little lighter than Rick, but he was a lot heavier on experience. He gave the blond-haired youngster a tough lesson in pro strategy. Bumping him, bouncing him, and elbowing him, he kept Rick off-balance—and off his game. Again and again he made the Warrior rookie look sad. As Warley crowed after the game, "I all but stuffed him in the basket."

Soon after that, Barry found himself matched against another bruising pro, Dave DeBusschere, then of Detroit. DeBusschere, one of the toughest and smartest forwards in the NBA, continued the rookie's education. He limited Rick to eight points while painting his body black-and-blue with a jarring defense that included the liberal use of elbows and shoulders. When asked later about Barry's prospects as a pro, the scornful DeBusschere said, "Barry should send away for some muscles. He can't push you out of the way, so he has to go around you. And we don't think he's that fast or maneuverable."

Slender and boyish-looking, Rick didn't seem capable of sustaining the run-and-bump game demanded by the long NBA schedule. But there was a lot more to Barry than met the eye, as he soon showed. The next time DeBusschere took on the Warrior rookie, Barry hit for 23 points in less than 30 minutes of play. DeBusschere changed his opinion in a hurry, as Rick displayed the kind of quickness and maneuverability that got him open for shots and the amazing accuracy that sank basket after basket.

Once he became confident that he could hold his own with the big-leaguers, Barry went on a scoring spree that made believers out of them all. Among the many he convinced was Dave Gambee of the Philadelphia 76ers. "High school kids look older than him," said the 76er regular, "and you tend to relax a little playing him. First time I did that he had 22 points off me—in two periods. He may be skinny, but once he has his hands on the ball, you don't get it away from him. He has great hands."

Rick also had courage and determination to go along with the hot-shooting hands that won him so many collegiate honors. Warrior owner Franklin Mieuli said, "Barry's as flexible as a whip, and a long time ago, when we scouted him in competition against the Russian national team, we saw how he reacts when somebody challenges him."

Warrior coach Alex Hannum was equally impressed. "One of the Russians got real tough with him," Hannum recalled, "and Rick came back with his best weapons. He began to hit on drives, jumpers, hooks—from everywhere—and ran up 14 points. The Americans won in overtime because of Rick, and we knew we had a draft choice who could take care of himself.

"Another thing about Rick is that he's never satisfied. After every game we play, even when he scores 40 points, he'll go home and think about the shot he missed and then go to practice and work on it so he won't miss again. Heck, Rick could be the first player never to miss a shot."

An exaggeration, of course. But Rick's search for basketball perfection was no exaggeration. It started back in Elizabeth, New Jersey, where Rick Barry III was born on March 28, 1944. His father, Rick Barry II, played semi-professional basketball for local club teams. And when he had time, he coached Rick's parochial grammar school team. Mr. Barry was a firm believer in the adage that "practice makes perfect," and in the evenings he practiced shooting and dribbling with Rick and his older son, Dennis. When the three Barrys weren't playing basketball, they talked about it.

"My mother had to tolerate it all," Rick recalled. "She didn't understand the game." As for his father, Rick said, "He was a strict fundamentalist and a strict disciplinarian. He drilled the fundamentals into me. You know—learn how to dribble without looking at the ball, learn how to pass, learn how to run backwards."

Rick never resented the strictness—in fact, he appreciated it. "The game was never forced on me," he said. "Always, I would get interested first.

I'd say, 'Show me,' and my father would show me. Take the way I shoot fouls. He taught me to shoot them underhand. He did not force me to do it that way. He just said, 'I'd like you to try it this way,' and he'd shoot fouls underhanded. I tried it, and it worked. I think I shoot five percent more fouls today because I shoot underhanded."

Rick sank a lot of foul shots—and two-pointers, as well—in his freshman year as a pro. In early April of that season he became the highest-scoring rookie forward in NBA history. His 2,059 points broke the mark set by super-great Elgin Baylor. When the annual NBA All-Star team was selected by the league writers and broadcasters at mid-season, Rick was the lone rookie on the squad. Playing for the first team, he contributed ten points, two assists, and two rebounds in 17 minutes of play.

At the end of the season the coaches named Barry as their only unanimous choice for the Rookie All-Star squad. Not surprisingly, he was Rookie of the Year, a pick that was almost automatic in view of his 25.7 points-a-game average and overall contributions for the Warriors.

The super-rookie became known as Super Soph in 1966–67. As an All-Star game superstar he blistered the basket for 38 points. Then he won the NBA scoring title, breaking Wilt Chamberlain's seven-year monopoly in that department. Wilt had cut down on his scoring to concentrate on defense and playmaking, as the Philadelphia 76ers went after the league championship. And, of course, Barry was one of the shooters that gave Wilt—and every other NBA defender—the toughest time. His season-long sharpshooting resulted in 2,775 points and a superb 35.6 points-per-game average.

Bill Sharman, who had replaced Alex Hannum as Warrior coach at the beginning of the season, was a Rick rooter all the way. "Rick is quicker than the big men who guard him," Sharman said, "and he can fake past them. Also, he is too big for the 'little' men like John Havlicek, who's two inches shorter than Rick. In addition, Rick has great body balance, is intelligent, and is a great competitor."

Rick had all that, plus an extraordinary shooting eye—especially when it came to shooting fouls the way his father had taught him. In one interview the free-throw wizard couldn't help boasting, "I can shoot fouls blindfolded." And when someone decided to put an end to his bragging by asking him to prove it, Rick proceeded to shut his eyes and sink six out of ten foul shots.

Some people found Barry's self-praise a little hard to take—even when he made good on his boasts. But Rick didn't see it as boasting. He explained his pride in his achievements by saying, "Whenever I want to do something, I always want to be best. I hate to be second best. I have a personal pride. I *like* to be best."

Rick Barry, the Warrior Super Soph, loses a rebound in a 1967 game against the Philadelphia 76ers.

Barry also wanted to be paid a lot more money, and after his excellent sophomore year he asked his Warrior bosses for a huge raise. When they didn't meet his demands, he jumped to the American Basketball Association's Oakland Oaks. However, he had signed a multi-year contract with the NBA club, and a California Superior Court ruled that Rick would play for the Warriors in 1967–68—or he would play for no one.

Rick chose to sit out the year. Then, just as he had predicted, he re-established his eminence as an incomparable scoring forward in the 1968–69 campaign. Hooking, driving, popping jumpers, and unleashing a torrent of free throws, Rick snared the ABA scoring crown with an average of 34 points a game. That made him the only basketball player in history to walk off with the scoring title in both pro leagues.

But not even Rick's eye-popping attacks on the basket could bring fans into the Oakland arena. The franchise folded after his first year with the club, and the Rick Barry Traveling Show was on the move again. He opened the 1969–70 season in Washington with the ABA's Capitols. San Francisco, Oakland, and now Washington, D.C. As it turned out, the Caps also lasted one year, giving Rick just enough time to pile up the highest average in the league for the second year in a row. This time, however, he failed to win the official scoring title because injuries had kept him from playing enough games to qualify for it.

In 1970 the Caps moved to Virginia, and changed the team name to the Squires. But Rick didn't want to be a Squire—or a gypsy. All this packing and unpacking was more than he could stand. He complained long and loud, and soon convinced his Virginia bosses to send him somewhere else. That somewhere else was New York, home of the ABA Nets. The Nets welcomed Rick, complete with his $125,000-a-year salary. After all, they said, it was a bargain price for the man with the golden hand.

Still troubled by a foot injury, Rick began the 1970–71 season slowly. But then he hit his stride and began a string of super-scoring nights. He hit for 35 against Indiana, collected two 41-pointers against Texas and Pittsburgh, and repeated against Pittsburgh with a basket-blasting outburst of 53 that included 34 points in the first half alone. His slow start blocked his path to another scoring crown, but he finished the year with a mark of 29.3 points a game, just a shade behind Dan Issel's league-leading 29.8.

Rick was often criticized for being a money-hungry showoff. But when his skills were measured, it wasn't hard to understand why teams in both leagues were fighting for the privilege of paying his salary. The Nets certainly knew his value. With

Playing for the New York Nets in 1970, Barry gets his shot off against Indiana's Bob Netolicky.

Barry in the line-up for 1971–72, New York had its best season ever. For the first time in their history the Nets finished a season with more wins than losses. Barry became a favorite with the fans, who came out in record numbers to watch him tear up the opposition. And he gave them quite a show. Scoring in dazzling numbers, he played in 80 games and swished in 2,518 points, good for second place in the scoring race. His 31.4 average was edged out this time by Charlie Scott's 34.5. But Rick was second to none in free-throw percentage. He hit 641 of 730 tries for a league-high .878 percentage. And for the fourth year in a row he was an ABA All-Star.

However, basketball's number one gypsy had to say goodbye to New York as far as the Nets were concerned. There was that little matter of a contract with the NBA's Warriors (still based near San Francisco but now known as the Golden State Warriors). After a long drawn-out court battle, the final legal word in the case of Rick Barry was, "Play for the Warriors—or no one."

Rick was back in a Warrior jersey when the '72 season began. But it was a "new" Rick Barry. Unlike the Barry of old, he was now telling everybody how happy he was to be back in the Bay Area. Barry didn't just sound different—he even looked different. When he'd left the Warriors in '66 Rick weighed 198 pounds, but now he pushed the scale's needle to 220. When Golden State faced the Knicks, there was Barry's old nemesis, Dave De-Busschere, then with New York. But this time, when the rough, tough, muscular DeBusschere began bumping and shoving Rick, he found Rick bumping and shoving right back.

There were other differences, too. The "Golden Gunner" didn't move quite as fast as he had five years earlier, but he had acquired many skills that more than made up for his slight loss of speed. So, when the Knicks tried to drive Barry outside, beyond his normal shooting range, he killed their strategy by sinking the Warriors' first two baskets on long-range jumpers. And when the Knicks collapsed on him, expecting him to go for his shot against their smothering defense, he fed his open teammates for easy buckets. Every now and then, just to keep the New York defense guessing, he drove past DeBusschere for left- and right-handed lay-ups as Golden State handed the Knicks a 127–104 defeat.

Rick explained that he had learned to be "a complete player," defensively as well as offensively, because "you had to do it all to win in the ABA." Warrior guard Jeff Mullins acknowledged his teammate's improved play but added, "It's also important to realize that defenses have changed since 1967. Defenses try to jam you now, try to overplay you, double up, sag, or do anything legal to change your pattern. The forwards are shorter;

the game is faster. And Rick is ideal for today's game. He's also more polished offensively than in '67. He doesn't go to the hoop as much because we have plenty of shooters. But he's a far better passer. In fact, I don't know of any forward who passes as well on the give-and-go."

Al Attles, who was then coaching the Warriors, was another big Barry booster. "Rick is still slick," he said, "and he has more muscle than he did in '67. We would have hesitated then to have him play a big guy like Elvin Hayes, but not now. I think he became a better player in the other league because he didn't have Nate Thurmond [the Warriors' outstanding defensive center] to depend on."

Playing a total game—passing, strong defense, scoring at a pace that better suited the team concept—Rick hushed the voices of doubters who had once called him big-mouthed, point-crazy, and money-hungry. His 1972–73 statistics were an ironclad argument against his harshest critics. While his scoring—a 22.3 average on 1,832 points in 82 games—was still impressive, it was only 13th in the league. It wasn't that his shooting eye had blurred any—Rick's first-place finish in the free-throw department (a percentage of .902) was clear evidence of that. No, it was because he had become the Warriors' top assists man, with 399 that season, and their second best rebounder, behind carom-master Nate Thurmond.

"When we need points," said a teammate, "Rick

Rick Barry: pro basketball's gypsy.

gets them for us. But now we know he's there to do all the other things a forward's supposed to do. It makes a big difference in team attitude."

Getting points is exactly what Barry did in Golden State's times of need during the 1973–74 campaign. A prime example was his marksmanship on December 8, 1973, in a fiercely contested Warrior-Laker game. Going into that game as his team's top assists man, Rick moved back into the role of super-scorer. Against the Lakers he blitzed the basket for 22 points on lay-ups and short-range jumpers. And when L.A. blocked his inside route, he used Nate Thurmond's towering body as a screen and bombarded the Lakers with another 20 points on outside one-handers. Adding eight-for-eight from the free-throw line, the Golden Gunner finished the night with 50 points (the tenth time he hit that milestone) spearheading the Warriors to a 135–111 victory.

As the Warriors continued to challenge the division-leading Lakers for first place—and a championship playoff berth—Barry's hot hand was needed more than ever. And he responded to that need. The "new" defense-oriented Barry may have begun the season, but after the All-Star break, it was the Golden Gunner all the way. From then on, he put the ball in the hoop at his old 30-points-a-game pace. Meanwhile, the Warriors won 20 out of 28 games to take over the division lead before being edged out by L.A. in the last week of the regular season.

Rick Barry had clearly developed into a triple threat—scorer, playmaker, and rebounder. Whatever the Warriors needed, he was ready, willing, and able to contribute. The Warriors hadn't won the championship that year, but if Barry had anything to say about it, they'd make it the next year . . . or the year after. For at long last, it seemed that the Rick Barry Traveling Show had found a home.

Walt Frazier

On-court or off-court, nobody in the NBA or ABA could match the stylishness of Walt Frazier. The New York Knickerbockers' All-Star backcourt ace was pro basketball's coolest hot shot.

In fact, Frazier was nicknamed "Mr. Cool," an image he purposely tried to project. As Frazier explained it, "I remember, in my rookie year, I was guarding Elgin Baylor. He just kept looking at me as if I wasn't there. I had no idea what he was thinking. It was great. I decided I would develop my style the same way. It's simple. You just can't reflect pressure in the pros. You can see it on a guy's face. If you see he's starting to crack or that the pressure is getting to him, you go at him all the harder. If he doesn't show the pressure, then you back off and try something else. That's why I always keep the cool, straight face. I don't ever let the man I'm guarding know if he's bothering me."

But more often than not, it was the man guarding Frazier who had to worry about keeping his cool. On-court, Walt was the grandmaster of ball-control. He worked with icy craftsmanship, a world apart from the explosive and unpredictable artistry of basketball's other hot shots. Frazier dribbled with a shrewd nonchalance that practically dared his rivals to try and take the ball away. He'd tap-tap-tap far in front of his body, bent low and balanced, set to shift in any direction with the fluid grace of an eel. Cutting across the court, he'd casually dribble-pass the ball behind his back without losing a beat. But just let a steal-hungry guard be tempted to snatch at the ball, and the slick Knick would whiz by him, buzzing in for a driving goal. Or if Frazier really wanted to dazzle the crowd, he'd ignore the easy jumper open to him and do the unexpected, wrist-flicking a pass to a cutting teammate for a sure two-pointer.

That was Walt's incomparable offensive style. On defense, he was also an A-one showman. Hounding a ball-handler, he became a cat-like hunter with hands as swift as any karate expert's, the long, strong fingers ready to snag the ball in the midst of a startled opponent's dribble.

Stealing the ball was one of Frazier's greatest

New York's Walt Frazier reaches out and steals the ball right out of the hands of Pistol Pete Maravich.

pleasures. It's the grandstand play of a hot shot because the fans love it and react with clapping, stamping, and whistling. "Do it, Clyde!" they'd yell. And he would, a cool grin showing between his muttonchop sideburns.

"Clyde" was another fitting nickname for Frazier. He earned that one away from the court, for the way he dressed in the latest, most expensive clothes. From head to toe, he was a fashion plate. One of the favorite items in his wardrobe was a wide-brimmed hat, the kind worn by gangsters back in the 1930's. Since Clyde Barrow (the famous bank robber immortalized in the movie *Bonnie and Clyde*) wore such a hat, Frazier became "Clyde" to one and all. And don't forget, he *was* basketball's most daring thief. "Clyde could steal the hub caps off a moving car," his fans loved to boast.

In a game, he was sharp and cool, playing a brand of basketball that paid off in points, steals, assists, and Knick victories. On the street, he was sharp and cool, wearing that eye-catching hat, alligator shoes, brightly colored clothes, and driving a plum-colored Rolls-Royce. In Madison Square Garden or around New York City, Clyde was a pace-setter without compare.

Life wasn't always so cool and easy for Walt Frazier. Born on March 29, 1945, in Atlanta, Georgia, he was the oldest of nine children. Walt was kept pretty busy taking care of his brothers and sisters, but he spent most of his spare time playing basketball.

Even as a child, Walt had a style of his own. From the time he was nine years old, going up against twelve-year-olds a foot taller, he decided that the best way to beat them at basketball was to do things differently, and do them better. Defense, he decided, was the secret. The big guys wanted to score, and he made it his job to stop them. He did it by getting in close and harrying them, making his confused opponents wonder what the fast and determined kid would do next. Frazier liked to score as much as the next guy, but he derived as much satisfaction from being a basketball thief or hitting the open man with a pinpoint pass.

On the playgrounds, he was a "class" player, and he didn't have to score in high figures to gain that distinction. Playing smart worked for him then, and it kept on working for him as a star athlete at Atlanta's Howard High School. A headline-making basketball player there, he was just as great on the football field. When Walt decided there was more pro promise for a black basketball player than a black quarterback, he started concentrating on the hoop sport. He refused football scholarship offers from such colleges as Indiana and Kansas. In fact, he turned down these same two schools—and many others—when they offered him basketball scholarships, and chose to attend lesser-known Southern Illinois University, in Carbondale, Illinois, instead.

The lure at SIU was basketball coach Jack Hartman. Hartman emphasized the defensive part of the game. "Most guys play defense straight up," Frazier said, "but with Hartman you learned to play in a crouch. He drilled us on this all the time. It was a reaction drill: left, right, back. We did it so much you couldn't straighten up. But if you didn't play defense for Hartman, you didn't play."

That was fine with Walt—defense had been his game long before he went to SIU. At 6-foot-4 and 200 pounds, Frazier was a "swing man" for Hartman's Salukis. If he was needed at a forward position, that's where he played. If his coach said, "Play guard," then he switched his thinking and action to the backcourt. In his junior year Frazier led the Salukis to a 20–2 season and a chance to play in the National Invitation Tournament championship. That competition ended with SIU the NIT champions and Walt the tournament's MVP. It also gave him a chance to show his stuff to the pro scouts who had come to size up potential prospects.

One of those men was Eddie Donovan, then the Knicks' general manager. "We were really impressed with Frazier's overall game," Donovan recalled. "He handled the ball well, had a great sense of direction, played fine defense. And on offense, if he wasn't in a good position to shoot, he'd give it to someone who was. We felt he had to be unusual."

The Knicks took Donovan's advice and picked Frazier on the first round of the 1967 college player draft. The SIU star was also drafted by the ABA, but he picked the Knicks because, he said, "they're on their way to a championship."

That championship didn't materialize until 1970, and Frazier's stardom didn't materialize right away, either. He didn't see too much playing time in his freshman season, when he averaged just nine points a game.

He calmly accepted the role of bench-rider, saying, "I knew I'd be sitting a lot as a rookie, and I realized in the beginning that I wasn't ready to move right in. I didn't have confidence in my shooting. If I missed a couple of shots, then I'd stop shooting. The thing you have to learn is not to let it bother you. You have to have confidence in your own ability. I was different from other rookies when I signed with the Knicks. Most guys have the offense and have to learn how to play defense. It was just the opposite with me. I played good defense, but I wasn't very sure of my offense.

Surrounded by the Lakers, Frazier hits the open man, Bill Bradley, with a perfect pass.

"Then about halfway through the season, everything just seemed to come together. Suddenly I started driving, penetrating, hitting the open man—all the things I knew I could do but hadn't been doing up to that time. I became the player I always knew I could be."

With Walt's growing confidence came the recognition of his peers. His playing time increased, and he was selected as one of the guards on the 1967 All-Rookie Team.

A backcourt starter the next season, Frazier gave rhythm to a team that badly needed a leader. And by helping to shape the New Yorkers until they finally grooved into a silky defensive unit, he became the main cog in the victorious Knickerbocker machine.

Clyde's defense was just part of his contribution. When the Knicks got the ball and headed for the other end of the floor, he turned into their masterfeeder. In 1968–69 he registered 635 assists (7.9 per game) to earn third place in the NBA assist race. He was second among guards in shooting percentage, connecting on 531 baskets out of 1,052 tries; and his 341 free throws boosted his tally to 1,403 points, for a per-game mark of 17.7. To top it all off, he pulled down 499 rebounds, prompting Cincinnati's Jerry Lucas (who later became a Knick teammate) to call Frazier "the best rebounding guard I've ever seen play this game."

Then came the 1969–70 season, the year the Knicks took it all. With All-Star forward Dave DeBusschere added to the line-up, the New Yorkers jelled into a defense-minded team that had their fans roaring "Deee-fense!" as they rolled to their first NBA championship in 24 years. And quarterbacking them was Frazier. In the words of one sportscaster describing the very hot Mr. Cool after a crucial Knick playoff victory, "What did Frazier do out there? What *didn't* he do? He passed, he saw, he shot, he stole the ball, he played defense. He did everything but serve lunch."

Frazier had been doing it all throughout that whole season. He finished his third pro campaign with a scoring average of 20.9 points a game. That wasn't all. He passed off repeatedly, garnering 629 assists for an 8.2 mark, good enough for second place behind league-leading Lennie Wilkens in that category. And if his steals had somehow been worked into the assists column, Wilkens would have been the runner-up.

The MVP award that championship season went to Frazier's teammate Willis Reed, but Walt didn't come away empty-handed. He was the top vote-getter on the NBA's list of All-Defensive players for the second year in a row, and he played his usual outstanding game as a starting guard in the All-Star contest.

Frazier's blazing play and unemotional face were

Walt Frazier: the New York Knicks' Mr. Cool.

a fire-and-ice combination that drove the fans wild. Clyde was their man, and they were his kind of audience. "There's no doubt a crowd can psych me up tremendously," he said. "I thrive on competition. I love the challenge. The more the crowd goes wild, the harder I play. Sometimes it's like something takes over inside. You make a steal and score. The crowd goes wild. I get turned on. I think I can steal everything. I wind up all over the floor, taking gambles. I get so psyched up I can't stay away from the ball."

Cool on the outside but burning like a bonfire inside, Clyde was a hard man to read. Mr. Cool made his spectacular moves look so effortless that his fans often took his four-star performances for granted. If Frazier merely had a good game, they grumbled because it wasn't great. After the Knicks once lost three in a row, and Frazier averaged "only" 19 points in those games, he was accused of loafing. Angrily, he answered his accusers, "A lot of people don't realize that scoring isn't my whole game. In fact, when I score 35 points, we're in trouble. That means I had to take over the offense. We win a lot more games when I score 20 points."

He went on, "A lot of people accuse me of dogging it until the fourth quarter and then turning it on. They think I'm deliberately grandstanding, setting it up like that so I can come on at the end like the Lone Ranger. But that's not true. People think I can score at will, but that's not true, either. I always play the second half better than the first because that's when most games are decided and lots of times I'll set things up defensively, like steals, and save them for the closing minutes, when

Double-teamed by the Bucks, Frazier goes up for his jump shot.

they have more of an impact. But that doesn't mean I dog it for the first three quarters."

Maybe it was the needling of his critics that got to him or maybe it was the need of the Knicks for more point production from their backcourt star; but whatever the reason, Clyde turned in the best offensive figures of his four-year career in 1970–71. Of course, he'd always had a keen eye for the basket, especially from the left side, 10 to 15 feet away from the hoop. He started the year by popping a lot more from his favorite spot, turning in several 30-points-plus performances in the process. Among his rooting section was Knick coach Red Holzman, who said, "Clyde has more confidence in his shooting now. He has become a good outside threat and that helps our shooting inside. He takes his shot now, when he should take it, and passes off when he should."

By the end of the season Frazier boasted a per-game average of 21.7 points. He also passed off for baskets 536 times, for a 6.7-assists-per-game average. And once again he was a member of the NBA's All-Star Team and All-Defensive Team. Even though the Knicks didn't retain their championship crown, it was clear that Clyde was still number one.

"I am the best all-around guard in the league," he told one reporter, and immodest as that may have sounded, few people disputed his claim. Even such reserved players as Knick teammate Bill Bradley spoke out publicly in Clyde's behalf. As Bradley said, "He's the only player I've ever seen I would describe as an artist, who takes an artistic approach to the game."

Frazier continued his backcourt artistry in 1971–72. With high-scoring Willis Reed injured for much of the season, Frazier carried more of New York's offensive burden and boosted his average to 23.2, a new personal high. He earned his perennial place on the NBA's All-Star Team and All-Defensive Team as he spearheaded the Knicks all the way to the championship finals against the Los Angeles Lakers.

The next season saw the Knicks back as NBA kings, with Mr. Cool calling the signals all the way. Defense was the key to their success, and Frazier, the man with the magic hands, was turning that key. Ball-hawking, his fingers flicked out to capture basketballs with the unerring accuracy and speed of a snake's tongue. His scoring was a steady 21.1 points a game, and he totaled 461 assists. Yet, because his scoring was two points below his previous season's mark, and his assists figure had dropped, his critics renewed their charge that Walt-the-Great was sloughing off.

Frazier's supporters responded by pointing out

that sharpshooter Earl Monroe (who had joined the Knicks in 1971–72) had picked up a lot of the scoring chores in the New York backcourt, along with dealing out passes for assists. But Frazier himself answered the knocks best when he said, "I still consider myself the best all-around player in basketball. Defensively I can control a game, and that's something no guard has ever done. I can't find any satisfaction in scoring 25 points and having my team come up a loser. There is a lot more to this game than just putting the ball in the basket.

"It's the man who wants to handle the ball in every clutch situation that you really need; the guy who wants to take the key shot, or go for the key steal. He's the one who'll win for you. The guy who comes up with ten baskets in the last quarter when the team is leading or trailing by 30 points is probably not going to be all that great when the pressure is hard."

During the first round of 1973–74 playoffs, Frazier got the perfect opportunity to show what he could produce in the clutch. With the Knicks and the Capitol Bullets tied in games with two apiece, Frazier put on a dazzling display in the fifth game of the series. He scored a sizzling 38 points, 16 of them in the crucial fourth quarter. He also had four assists and six rebounds, an all-around effort that gave the Knicks a 106–105 victory—and the inspiration that led them into the semifinals against the Boston Celtics. But even Frazier couldn't do everything. Plagued by injuries to their big men, Willis Reed and Dave DeBusschere, the Knicks finally bowed to Boston. Of course, Frazier was disappointed—but he was already thinking of the next season and another run for the championship. He wanted all the things that went along with the NBA crown: the glory, the awards, and the money that paid for his stylish clothes and luxury cars. But most of all, he wanted to be remembered as a "class" player. No problem there—Walt Frazier was truly the Rolls-Royce of pro basketball.

George McGinnis

They called him the Baby Bull. Looking at the bulging muscles that gave George McGinnis the appearance of a modern-day Atlas, it was impossible to imagine anyone mistaking him for a baby *anything*. But there was no questioning the Bull half of his nickname. Not when that powerful 6-foot-8, 235-pound body came thundering upcourt. It was enough to make any rival think twice before moving in to intercept him. As one opponent said after mixing it up with the indestructible McGinnis under the backboards, "You just can't let him get inside on you. He's so strong, he ought to be outlawed. He posts you underneath and just overpowers you."

These words were spoken during the 1971–72

season, McGinnis's rookie year with the ABA's Indiana Pacers. After leaving Indiana University as a sophomore, the young forward had hit the league with the impact of a bulldozer. "I like the pro game," big George remarked after one particularly grinding contest. "I like it physical with the body contact. They wouldn't let me play that way in college. They called me for charging.

"I like going inside, knocking a few people around and coming out with the ball—you can't score without it. And when I get up in the air, I like to wait until I feel contact before I shoot. That way I can get the foul, too."

Appearing in 78 games as a first-year Pacer, George piled up plenty of points, plenty of rebounds—and plenty of mistakes. His play was unpredictable. Coming into the big time with so little experience, he committed many wrong moves on the court—fouling opponents unnecessarily, losing the ball on careless maneuvers against fast-handed veterans, and forcing up low-percentage shots when he was out of position. There was no doubt that McGinnis had the potential to be a big-league star, but it would take some time before he could live up to that potential. Fortunately, his coach, Bob Leonard was willing to give him that time. Mistakes or not, Leonard stayed with him. Even when critics asked why he kept McGinnis in the line-up, especially after the Baby Bull had goofed in several games, the coach insisted, "George is coming along all the time. He's learning fine."

The mistakes didn't disappear, but he learned enough to average 16.9 points a game that first season, and to pull down 711 rebounds. Then George came through with better than 15.5 points and 10 rebounds a game in the playoffs as Indiana won the league crown. McGinnis' tireless, battering-ram efforts earned him a spot on the ABA All-Rookie Team, alongside another upcoming star forward named Julius Erving.

It was quite a beginning for George McGinnis. Fresh off the campus of Indiana University, he could boast about round-the-league cheers for his rookie play—and a championship ring. He wasn't much concerned about his faults—they'd disappear in time. After all, sports and sports success had always been part of his life.

Born on August 12, 1950, in Birmingham, Alabama, George was two years old when his family moved to Indianapolis, Indiana. His father earned a fairly good living as a construction worker, so there was plenty of food for George, a big healthy kid who could pack away huge meals.

Growing bigger and stronger each year, George developed the build of a weightlifter. And Indianapolis was the perfect place for a boy with his physical abilities to live. One of America's sports centers, the city prides itself on the large number of basketball and football stars it produces. George was one of the city's finest in both sports, and he also found time for other energetic pastimes, such as swimming. "There were a lot of swimming holes around," he recalled, "and I loved to swim and go boating. We weren't poor, but we couldn't afford a boat. It didn't matter, though—there was always a friend to take me out in his."

George's first love was basketball, and more than anything he wanted to be a professional basketball player. It was a dream that began when he was four, and it never faded. That possibility—and the possibility of a career in pro football—grew closer to reality as he gained a national reputation in both sports as a high-school athlete. A tall, fast, pass-catching end, he was chosen for the All-America high-school team. When he graduated from Washington High School more than 200 colleges wanted him to play football for them. But basketball was still his favorite game, and he brushed aside the scholarship offers by declaring, "Football's too rough."

It was hard to imagine any sport being too rough for the young man with the tank-like body. Basketball wasn't too rough for him, but it certainly must have been for anyone trying to get between him and the ball. In his senior year, George and his Washington High teammates had hammered out a

31–0 record before going on to win the Indiana state championship.

Even before graduation, George made up his mind to play college basketball right near home, at Indiana University. However, before heading for the IU campus, he topped off his high-school basketball career in the annual series between teams representing Indiana and Kentucky.

In the opening game of that match, George dominated the rebounding and went over the 20-point mark in scoring. But the Kentucky-Indiana rivalry was a long-standing, bitter one, and one of the Kentucky players tried to psych out George by telling a sportswriter, "McGinnis is overrated. He's not nearly as tough as he's cracked up to be."

If the Kentucky high-schooler was trying to intimidate McGinnis, he used the wrong approach. "I got really angry," George recalled. Translating his anger into action, he mutilated the other team with 53 points and 30 rebounds in the next game. There had been many prominent players in this series, including Oscar Robertson, Wes Unseld, and Tom and Dick Van Arsdale. But nothing they had ever done could measure up to the one-man wrecking job George McGinnis turned in that night.

Indiana U. could hardly wait for George to start doing the same wondrous things for its basketball team, but low college-board marks made him ineligible to play as a freshman. Still, he brought basketball fame to the school before he ever put on its uniform. At the end of his freshman year George joined a group of college players on a State Department-sponsored tour of Europe. Among his teammates were future pros Jim McDaniels, Jim Cleamons, John Mengelt, and Cliff Meely. The rest were juniors and seniors, but freshman George outplayed every one of them.

The off-season tour reached its peak when the college squad played a pair of exhibition contests against the NBA's Baltimore Bullets. George outscored and outrebounded his more experienced teammates, and refused to be intimidated by the pros. As he proudly proclaimed, "The Bullets had guys like Wes Unseld, Gus Johnson, and John Tresvant, and I was holding my own with them on the boards."

Coming from a player who had yet to see action in his first college game, it was a brash statement. There was little doubt that those combat-hardened pros could have taught George a few lessons and put the crunch on him if they'd wanted to. But perhaps they respected the cocky young player's talents and confidence enough to let him get away with both body and ego undamaged. Then, too, they might have studied George's power-packed frame and decided to save *themselves* from some bone-shaking bumps.

Playing for Indiana University, George McGinnis fakes his Ohio State defender off his feet.

Whether or not he was ready to challenge the big-league "heavies," George definitely was ready to take on the best competition Indiana had to face. As a sophomore, playing his first (and last) season of college ball, George led the Big Ten conference in scoring with a 29.9 average and in rebounding with almost 15 caroms a game.

George's classroom performance wasn't nearly up to his basketball heroics. Even so, he might have stayed on at Indiana if two factors hadn't shaped his future. First of all, his father was killed in an accident, and while his family was getting along on the insurance money, life was far from easy for them. Second, there were increasing rumors about a future merger between the NBA and ABA. If that happened, a college player entering the pros could expect far less money.

After his impressive sophomore season, George learned that the NBA's Phoenix Suns and Chicago Bulls wanted him to join them right away. Then he heard from the ABA's Indiana Pacers, who offered him the chance to play in his own hometown for a three-year contract worth $350,000.

McGinnis felt the Pacer package was just too good to turn down. "I wasn't a hardship case," he said after the signing. "I didn't have to turn pro for my family. The insurance money was adequate after my father died. But I didn't want to get devalued when and if the leagues merged."

His value was enormous, as the Pacers quickly learned. As soon as he began barreling up and down the courts, rival forwards learned to respect him, too. That didn't mean they let up in the slam-bang battles for rebounds. But that didn't bother George. He took the elbows, hips, and shoulders in stride, grunting and giving at least as much as he got.

George had no reason to regret his early jump to the big league, although he did miss the opportunity to win an NCAA championship. Had he stayed at the university, he would have been a senior member of the squad that played UCLA in the semifinals. With McGinnis in the line-up, Indiana U. just might have had a shot at halting Bill Walton and the Bruins' win-streak in 1972.

"I saw the game on television," McGinnis said. "It had a bit of an effect on me. But I don't know for sure if I could have stuck it out at Indiana. Bobby Knight took over as head coach, and I know if I could have adapted to his style we would have had a great time. But that's a big 'if.' He believes in moving the ball around quite a bit, waiting for the good shot and then putting it up. Well, I believe in taking the good shot, too, but I also believe in getting it off as soon as possible. I don't like to play around with the ball."

His shoot-fast, hit-hard style was a major factor as the Pacers took the championship in his rookie season. And instead of a possible trophy for winning the NCAA title as a collegian, he had a star-sapphire, 18-diamond ABA championship ring. "That's what it's all about," he said, grinning. "Winning. The first time is the best. The others will be good, too, but there's something about that first one that really turns you on."

It was the perfect ending for his rookie season, but McGinnis knew he would have been an even better pro player if he'd had more college ball experience. "I led the league in errors this year," he admitted with uncharacteristic modesty. "I guess that tells you that I'm in too much of a hurry." Then his confidence immediately returned and he added, "But everything started falling into place the more I played. And the more I play, the better I'm going to be."

There were other remarks he made that declared how highly he thought of himself. For example, when he was asked to compare himself with Julius Erving, McGinnis said, "I don't like to make comparisons between players. I'm not the type of guy who says 'I'm better than him or he's better than me.' If a guy can make it here in our league, then I'm all for him. Julius is a good ballplayer. In time he's going to be one of the super players of all basketball. But truthfully, he wouldn't be starting if he was with us. Look at our front line. Mel Daniels, me and Roger Brown. I don't think he could fit in there."

In other words, George was saying that the potential superstar, Julius Erving, wouldn't be good enough to push him out of the line-up. And he paid no attention to the countless voices that laughed in disagreement.

Big talk? Yes. Except that it would have taken an All-Star like Erving to dim George's rising star as far as scoring and rebounding were concerned. In the 1972–73 campaign, in which Indiana repeated as league champions, George finished right behind the league-leading Dr. J. in the scoring race. His second-place figures were 2,261 points for 82 games, an outstanding average of 25.5. And George finished *two* rungs higher than Erving on the rebounding ladder, taking fourth place with an average of 12.4 a contest. In addition, he was the sixth-leading player in steals, with 160—a pretty impressive accomplishment for a big forward.

Unfortunately, there was still another category in which George was ahead of Dr. J.—and Erving was glad to let him have it. In his sophomore season the Pacer frontcourt star had made more errors that resulted in turnovers than any other ABA player. As one writer described George's woeful distinction, "Until least season, the ABA record for errors was 356, set by Larry Brown.

George McGinnis: the Indiana Pacers' Baby Bull.

McGinnis didn't just break Brown's record. He smashed it. Ruined it. He committed 401 errors, an average of more than five a game."

A proud athlete, George set to work on cutting down his mistakes while building his scoring and rebounding totals ever higher. Rewarding Coach Leonard's faith in him, the third-year forward not only maintained his dramatic scoring, he exceeded it when the Pacers needed more points. In the middle of the 1973–74 season center Mel Daniels was forced to the sidelines by injury, so Mighty McGinnis stepped up his point production. In one six-game stretch he rang up totals of 37, 29, 44, 27, 24, and 25. At the same time, he didn't slack off in his rebounding, grabbing 25, 29, 17 and 21 caroms in four of those high-scoring affairs.

The peak of his solo super-effort came on January 12, 1974. Taking on the Carolina Cougars front line in what amounted to a one-man offense–defense, McGinnis shelled the hoop for 52 points and snared a whopping 37 rebounds. His backboard work that night set a regular-season record, breaking the single-game rebounding mark of 35 established by Manny Leaks in 1970. No one—including the fabulous Wilt Chamberlain or Bill Russell—had ever compiled such an amazing total of points and rebounds in a single game.

With each succeeding year, McGinnis was getting better and better—and stronger and stronger. Early in George's career, ABA forward John Baum said it for every forward, then and afterward: "That man is just too strong to be playing basketball. The man should be a heavyweight contender. No, make that a heavyweight champion."

No, make that a basketball champion. Because that was what George McGinnis was determined to be—the best rebounder-scorer ever. And as his rivals already knew, when the Baby Bull wanted something, he was a hard man to stop.

Spencer Haywood

"Basketball saved me from becoming an alcoholic or an addict or a hood," said Spencer Haywood, the Seattle SuperSonics' biggest superstar. "When I got into it, I could see it was the way out for me."

What Haywood wanted to escape was the grinding poverty into which he was born. His father died a month before Spencer was born on April 22, 1949. That left his mother with a house full of kids (Spencer was her ninth child) and no money to feed them. So she began scrubbing floors for $10 a week to add to the $10 welfare money she received from the government. It was a barren, dreary, hungry existence the Haywood family lived in Silver City, Mississippi.

"Our house was clean," Spencer remembered,

"but it was old, raggedy, decaying. We slept three in a bed. The worst thing was going to bed hungry. It hurt in your gut. The only thing worse was waking up hungry and knowing there wasn't any food to take that hunger away from you. We'd cut wood, make the fire, get out in the fields and pick cotton. I started when I was six. I'd pick up to 200 pounds a day. I wasn't very good. I did it to survive, not to break world records. I got two dollars a hundred, four dollars a day. People would pass out in the fields from sunstroke. The temperature would hit a hundred and ten."

The fury that blazed inside the young boy was almost as hot as the scorching fields. And the struggle to survive shaped him into a person tough enough to hit out at anything or anyone who blocked his path to escape. The world was his enemy and he was ready at an early age to do anything necessary to defeat it. "When I was a kid," he said, "I was treated like a dog. It gives you ambition, once you get out, to do something."

The first thing he did was to get away from Silver City. A poor student there, he was no better when he moved in with relatives "up North" in Chicago. Spencer got a different education on the big-city streets, where he and his gang hung out. As he recalled it, years after he had battered through the barriers of the slum world, "I was, you know, a thug. All I wanted to do was rob people, or hustle a pool game, whatever it took to make some money."

After a summer in Chicago, Haywood moved to Detroit. It was there that his dreams for a better life started to become a reality. And it was there that he met Will Robinson, a man who helped him turn his life around.

Robinson, then the basketball coach at Detroit's Pershing High School, became Spencer's guardian and convinced him to stop running along the gangster path that would, sooner or later, land him in jail—or an early grave. And to give the 15-year-old street-wise kid a sound family environment, Robinson arranged for him to move in with a Detroit couple named Mr. and Mrs. Bell, who became his joint guardians.

The Bells had two sons of their own and Spencer was treated like a member of the family. His improved home situation plus the friendship and coaching of Will Robinson inspired Haywood to take a serious approach to school and basketball. And very quickly Spencer learned that he didn't have to steal the things he wanted—he could earn them.

Spencer worked hard in the classroom and on the basketball court. He raised his D average to a B. And if they gave grades for basketball, he would surely have gotten an A-plus there. Haywood became an All-America high-school star and in his senior year he led Pershing to the Michigan state

Spencer Haywood (8) intimidates a Brazilian rival in the '68 Olympics.

championship. He then enrolled at Trinidad Junior College in Colorado, where his average of 27 points and 23 rebounds a game brought him an invitation to try out for the 1968 U.S. Olympic squad. He made the team, becoming the youngest U.S. basketball competitor in Olympic history. The 19-year-old collegian turned out to be the moving force behind the United States' successful bid for a gold medal.

Haywood's spectacular Olympic performance was reported in newspapers all over the country. All the experts agreed that he would someday be a pro star.

Meanwhile, Haywood had transferred to the University of Detroit, where he immediately began to live up to his rave notices. In his very first varsity game, the powerful forward slammed the ball through the hoop so forcefully that he completely shattered the backboard. The basket didn't count because dunking wasn't allowed in college, but that awesome display of super-strength thrilled the fans anyway.

After that dynamic demonstration Spencer's stock soared, and so did the school's. At one point his team was ranked seventh nationally. Then Detroit started losing some games, and the next thing to stun the school, Spencer's coach, and the NBA, was the news that Haywood was joining the Denver Rockets of the ABA.

The powerful 21-year-old was an instant success as a pro. In his first game he was thrown into a situation that would have paralyzed most rookies—a head-on clash with the defending ABA champions, the Washington Capitols. Nervous but determined, the rookie center played uncertainly in the opening minutes. Then he blended smoothly into the tempo of the game and started pouring it on. Hitting the boards hard and often, he snared rebounds with his massive hands and zipped passes to teammates for the fast break.

A natural shooter from the start, Haywood worked hard on his defense and stated his desire to be as much like Bill Russell as possible. "Russell has been my hero for as long as I can remember," Haywood said. "I've read his books on basketball and everything he's said that I could find. I've followed his career since I was old enough to read. He's my idol. The thing is, I've got to assume his responsibility on defense. It's something that will take time, but that's what I'm aiming for."

Haywood's great show of strength at the beginning of his freshman season barely hinted at the feats he would accomplish before the 1969–70 schedule ended. In one game against the L.A. Stars, Haywood poured in 59 points to break the league's single-game scoring mark of 57, set by Connie Hawkins in his ABA days. As play-by-play announcer Sam Balter declared, "Spencer Haywood is on his way to developing into the perfect player. He's a composite of all those people we call superstars."

Later in the season, Haywood got a chance to test himself against all those superstars when he

An ABA All-Star in 1968–69, Haywood gets off a shot for the West.

was named to the ABA All-Star Team. Playing combat-style basketball against big Mel Daniels, the league's 1968–69 MVP, Spencer snared 19 rebounds to Daniels' 12, and outscored Mel 23 to 13. Haywood's sterling play led his West team to a 30-point win and earned him the game's MVP award.

By the time the regular season was in the books, Haywood had lifted the third-place Rockets to the top of the Western Division and established himself as the league's top star. He scored the most points of any player in the ABA (2,519) for a league-leading average of 29.9 points per game. He also hauled down the most rebounds (1,637), an average of 19.4 per game. It came as no surprise when Haywood took home two trophies at the close of the year—one for Rookie of the Year, and one for Most Valuable Player in the ABA.

At the age of 21, Spencer Haywood was already acknowledged as one of basketball's biggest stars. He had come a long way from the Mississippi fields where he'd picked cotton for four dollars a day as a six-year-old, but he still wasn't happy. He felt he wasn't being paid what he was worth and, more disturbing to him, he believed the Denver Rockets' owners were treating him "like a slave." As Haywood told a reporter, "At Denver, they practically said to me, 'We own you. You will take what we give you and you will be thankful.'"

The relationship of the reigning king of the ABA and his bosses went from miserable to unbearable. Unable to come to terms with them, Spencer jumped to the NBA's Seattle SuperSonics. There he felt he could get more money, more respect, and better competition.

Denver tried to stop Haywood from playing for the rival league and challenged his jump to the NBA. The result was a series of court battles that kept Spencer sidelined until a judge finally ruled that he was entitled to play wherever he wanted to. However, the legal involvement cost Haywood a lot of playing time, and he didn't get to play until the last part of the 1970-71 season.

The transition from the ABA to the NBA was a difficult one, and Haywood got off to a slow start in his new league. He was 6-foot-8 and weighed 230 pounds, yet he was bounced around like a rubber ball by such goliaths as centers Wilt Chamberlain, Nate Thurmond and Bob Lanier, and such steel-hard forwards as Gus Johnson and Dave DeBusschere. Still, he knew that it was just a matter of time before he would adapt to the NBA style of play.

"That's why I switched to this league from the ABA," Haywood said. "In the ABA, the whole game is run and shoot. Here, it's defense. It is physically different. Each night you meet a good team. Each night you have to play a good tight, tough defense. I want to play guys like that, teams like that. It brings out the most in me. I love competition. I love the physical quality of the game."

Haywood adjusted quickly enough to average 20.6 points and 12 rebounds in the 33 games he played that season. In that short time he impressed a lot of NBA players and coaches. Los Angeles Laker coach Bill Sharman said, "What is he now, 21, 22 years old? Right now he should be just a rookie in this league, but he's ahead of rookies because he's been playing pro. He's made a big jump now, and he has to get adjusted and figure out how to use best the things he does best. But he has as much going for him as any man who ever came into this game, and he could become the greatest."

Haywood was pleased with Seattle as a city, with the team's owner, Sam Schulman, and most of all with his coach, Lenny Wilkens. He described Wilkens in the same glowing words he had used for Bill Russell: "Lenny is my idol," Haywood said. "He never gives me a break in practice. He runs me the whole time. I like it. If I'm going to play 44, 45 minutes in a regular game, I've got to get in shape."

Wilkens saw Haywood as a good player who had a chance to be great. And the Seattle player-coach was eager to work with the new Sonic. "He does a

Playing with the Seattle SuperSonics, Spencer is about to score despite the efforts of Wilt Chamberlain.

lot of things naturally," Wilkens said, "but he has a lot of skills to learn that have to be learned. He wants to learn. He's very coachable. He's not one of those guys who thinks he knows it all already. Too many guys want it easy. We got some on this team. He's not that way."

Through the opening weeks of his first full NBA season (1971–72) Spencer averaged 25 points and 15 rebounds a game. He also blocked shots at a rate of close to five a contest. Yet he wasn't playing the kind of defense he knew he was capable of playing, and his rivals were scoring on him at a rate close to his own point production. On top of that, he was being called for a great many fouls, and his frustration led to a series of explosive reactions. Again and again, he would scream at referees, accusing them of unfairness and claiming that they were picking on him. He also unloaded his anger on opposing players, and he even threw punches at several of them.

Still, his raw talent drew as much praise as his raw temper drew criticism. At one point during the season, Jerry West said, "He's just on the verge of dominating games. It's hard for him because his team doesn't have a top center and he has to take on the big centers. But he can jump out of sight, and he's got moves that won't stop. And he's very strong and tough and talented."

Bit by bit, Haywood's hot temper cooled, and he

even reached the stage where he could view his flaring tantrums with objectivity. "I had a negative point of view," he admitted. "I've changed my attitude. I've matured. I don't dispute calls. The ref says, 'You fouled,' and I say, 'Yes, I did. I won't foul him again.' I deal with the referee this way."

Still as hot as ever with a basketball in his hands, Spencer wrapped up the 1971–72 season with a batch of gold stars on his NBA report card. He was the league's fourth best scorer, with a per-game average of 26.2 points, and his board-work, close to 13 rebounds a game, fell just below the league's top ten in that department. He got the NBA's stamp of approval by being voted to the mid-season All-Star squad, and at the end of the season he was named to the league's All-Star first team.

Still, there was room for improvement, as he showed in 1972–73. His 29.2 points-per-game pace made him the third best scorer in the league, and his 12.9 caroms a contest earned him tenth place in the rebounding race. Again Spencer was an All-Star game participant and one of the two forwards on the 1973 All-Star first team.

The devastating play of young Spencer Haywood captivated many sportswriting veterans of the basketball beat. Among them was Phil Elderkin, who wrote, "Haywood is one of those marvelously coordinated big men who can do almost everything a little man can do. He's fluid on the

Haywood cools off on the sidelines after another hot-scoring game.

drive, strong inside, and a natural rebounder. Among today's top players, he easily answers 'yes' to the questions: Can he run? Can he score? Can he rebound? Can he defend? If you were starting a new team and had first shot at the game's best forwards, chances are you'd go for Haywood first."

Playing forward when his team needed him there, Haywood did the job. And when the Sonics needed him at center, he filled that post admirably. Wilkens was no longer coaching then, but he was replaced first by Tom Nissalke, and then by the immensely shrewd and talented Bill Russell. Haywood's super-hero had become his coach, and that could only mean even greater things for Spencer and the SuperSonics.

Wherever and however Russell wanted him to play, that's where and how Spencer played. The brutal early years were far behind him, and so were the difficult break-in seasons in the NBA. Spencer Haywood had changed from a hot-headed kid into a hot shot superstar.

Geoff Petrie

The Portland Trail Blazers hurried upcourt on February 13, 1971. The center set up at the top of the key, while the forwards headed for the corners. At the same time, rookie guard Geoff Petrie brought the ball across the midcourt line, shifting direction against the skin-tight defensive efforts of Seattle guard Dick Snyder. Suddenly, Petrie's medium speed became jet-propelled as he blurred past Snyder toward the foul line. As Portland's big men collapsed toward the basket, muscling for rebound position, the Blazer rookie came to an abrupt stop 15 feet from the hoop and quickly released a one-handed jumper. There was no rebound for the big men to fight for as the ball dipped through the basket, barely rippling the net.

Moments later, Petrie's teammate Stan McKenzie stole a Seattle pass and snapped it over to Geoff. Petrie bounced the ball once, soared into the air, and released the shot. The long-range bomb arched high and plunged into the hoop.

Up and down the court the two teams raced, treating Portland's hometown rooters in Memorial Coliseum to a breathtaking show of run-and-gun basketball. The game ended with Portland on top, 137–125, and much of the Trail Blazers' fiery display of scoring power came from the 6-foot-4, 200-pound Petrie. The unstoppable rookie had poured in almost a third of his team's points, registering a total of 43 on a variety of drives, one spectacular dunk shot at the end of a fast break, ten long-range jumpers, and a bunch of foul shots.

Dick Snyder, noted for his clinging defensive play, was upset—but not very surprised—by his own inability to stem Petrie's flow of points. For several weeks earlier, the SuperSonic guard had had similar difficulties when Geoff had hit for 40 points. "I think I can stay with him," Snyder said gloomily, "but he just seems to shoot better if I'm hanging all over him."

Seattle's player-coach, Lennie Wilkens, understood his teammate's dismay. Wilkens, one of the league's premier guards in the 1960's and '70's, agreed that 22-year-old Petrie was one of the best rookies in the NBA. But then Wilkens added, "He has great moves and an almost unstoppable jump shot. I consider him one of the finest shooters around. People talk about Petrie as a rookie. I think it is time to talk about him as a player."

Around the circuit, a lot of hard-to-impress insiders were singing the same kind of praise. Petrie was truly amazing by rookie standards, but even against the league's experienced veterans, the young guard could more than hold his own. Following a typical Petrie scoring outburst against Detroit, the Pistons' coach, Bill van Breda Kolff, said, "Petrie has one of the quickest jump shots in the game. He can stop on a dime after going full-bore, rock back, and fire a shot that's almost impossible to block."

And Dave Bing, Detroit's All-Star guard, added, "He *is* a star in this league. I don't think he's just going to be. He probably has the best range of any backcourt man—any player at any position, for that matter—in the game."

After a Blazer victory over Philadelphia, two of the 76ers reluctantly added their names to the Petrie fan club. Fred Crawford admitted, "He hit three jumpers in a row off me that I didn't even see. He seemed to be dribbling, and faking with his head, and the next thing I know, the ball is in the hoop." Crawford's teammate, Wally Jones, agreed by saying, "When he's hitting that jump shot, there's nothing you can do but count 'em up."

It was a lot of praise for a rookie, but it was well deserved—and long overdue. Petrie, born April 17, 1948, had received very little national recognition before his NBA debut. A native of Springfield, Pennsylvania, his biggest distinction had been as a high school All-America. And although he was outstanding in his varsity play with Princeton, he was overshadowed by such highly publicized college stars as Pete Maravich, Bob Lanier, and Calvin Murphy. Princeton's Ivy League schedule wasn't considered a tough testing ground for a basketball player, and not even the fact that Bill Bradley (who later became a Knick star) had played for the Tigers immediately before Petrie's arrival could impress the followers of college basketball. But Portland, an expansion team beginning its first year in the NBA, was impressed enough with Petrie to grab him on the first round of the 1970 college draft.

Petrie hit the NBA like a locomotive that just kept on gathering steam. Not many guards could handle him, and only on rare off-nights did the Blazer basketeer fail to sink at least 20 points. He scored 40 or more in six games, 30 or more in 22 games, and 20 or more in 59 games. His game high was a scorching 46 points. In addition to all that scoring, he also led the club in assists, with 390, the fourth-highest total ever for an NBA rookie.

With those credentials he should have had a lock

Portland's Geoff Petrie fires the shot which made him the seventh rookie in NBA history to pass the 2,000-point mark.

on the Rookie of the Year award. But two other first-year men were having pretty good seasons themselves—Dave Cowens, the Boston Celtics' young super-center, and Atlanta's sharp-shooting Pete Maravich. Not only did they have the advantage of playing for teams that were far more successful than the Portland entry, they also received much wider attention from newspapers, magazines, and television. But even though Cowens and Maravich got tons of publicity, Petrie couldn't be totally ignored. When the ballots cast by sportswriters and broadcasters were counted, Maravich had come in third, while Cowens and Petrie had tied for Rookie of the Year.

It was the first time in NBA history that the award had to be shared. As far as Portland's coach, Rolland Todd, was concerned, "Geoff would have had it all to himself if he'd been playing for an Eastern team, where a player gets more exposure. Anyway, award or no award, Geoff wants to be the best, and I think he will be. He's the kind of player who can turn a game around."

Geoff had no complaints about his half-share in the award, but he was even more honored by a compliment he got from Jerry West. After an explosive Petrie effort against the great Laker guard, West said, "I think we just saw the birth of a new superstar. Geoff scored 35 points in 31 minutes—an outstanding performance!"

When told about West's remark, Petrie said, "It

doesn't embarrass me to admit that I am a great fan of West. In a way, I owe my jump shot to him. I patterned my shooting style after West's. Until my junior year at Princeton, I wasn't much of a jump-shooter . . . more of a driver. But I realized I'd have to develop a better outside shot. So I watched West on television one Sunday and marveled at the quickness with which he got his shot away. I saw how he takes a real hard dribble just before he shoots, so the ball bounces higher and quicker into his hands for the jump shot. That's what I did. Now when I maneuver for a shot, I always take the hard dribble before I leave the floor. The ball naturally gets up to my hands quicker, and I'm ready to release it a lot faster."

There didn't seem to be much room for improvement in Petrie's shooting, but coach Todd worked to help his rookie develop as an all-around player. "In the beginning," Todd said, "when he was sorting things out and learning how to play the pro game, he would revert to a one-on-one, run-and-gun style when we needed points."

Todd warned Petrie that other teams would concentrate their defense on a hot shot, knowing that he would try to score every time he got the ball, and urged Geoff to think about team play, too. Petrie paid attention, and soon Todd was saying, "Now he sees the open man more. He passes off more when he gets double-teamed. And he has found out how to move effectively without

Petrie goes up for a jumper against Cincinnati's Dick Van Arsdale.

the ball and how to let his teammates set him up for higher percentage shots."

As Petrie improved, so did the Trail Blazers. And although they finished their first season with only 29 wins and 53 losses, they had the best record of the three new expansion teams. (Buffalo and Cleveland had also entered the league that year.)

The 1971–72 season opened with Geoff gunning to make his second pro campaign even starrier than his first. But two things ruined his plans. Number one was a knee operation that hampered his movements and limited his scoring to just under 19 points a game. The second was Sidney Wicks, the Trail Blazers' newest draft choice. Wicks, a big, strong forward from UCLA, had tremendous firepower. An immediate rivalry sprang up between the two big scorers.

Although Wicks didn't actually use Petrie's name, there was no doubt that he felt Geoff's constant shooting was behind Portland's poor showing that season. "I'm saying that some people are playing team ball," Wicks told a reporter, "and some people aren't. With the team we have, we can play with anyone in the league, but we can't do that with the guys doing what they're doing right now. There are too many guys out there playing for themselves—guys dribbling around with their heads down, not looking for other guys."

Presumably, Geoff was the guy "dribbling

around" and Sidney was the "other guy" Geoff should have been looking for. Petrie responded by saying that Wicks "was just as guilty as anybody else" when it came to playing for personal glory. However, Geoff was willing to add, "I'll take a lot of the blame, too. Something's got to be done or we won't win another game the rest of the year."

Not enough could be done, even though Wicks and Petrie tried to share the scoring chores from then on. Despite its sparkling pair of point-makers, Portland finished the season with a dismal 18–64 record, the worst in the league.

The team improved a bit in 1972–73, mainly on the strength of Petrie's further development as a total player. His defense, something every pro newcomer must learn, was steadily getting tougher. But more than that, he established himself as the leader of the club. During his third season Petrie averaged 24.9 points a game, taking seventh place in the league scoring race. He could have registered an even higher average, but many times—putting the team ahead of himself—he fed off to Wicks and other players instead of taking the shot himself. That enabled Wicks to finish ninth in NBA scoring, gave Portland better balance—and stopped a lot of critics from calling Geoff "the Blazer ball-hog."

In the spring of 1973, however, Geoff had a chance to do his thing for a nationwide TV audience—and not get blasted by teammates and

This time Geoff can't get the shot off as he is fouled by the Philadelphia 76ers' Fred Carter.

critics for showing off. That was when he became involved in a one-and-one contest against the top man-to-man players in the league. Elimination rounds knocked out such super-scorers as Bob McAdoo, Spencer Haywood, and Gail Goodrich, but Geoff just kept sailing along. And when the one-on-one king of the NBA was decided in the final round, none other than Geoff Petrie walked off wearing the crown.

Kareem Abdul-Jabbar

For all of Kareem Abdul-Jabbar's height (the record book listed him as 7-foot-2, but he soared closer to 7-foot-4) and weight (230 pounds), the Milwaukee Bucks' center looked like a huge spider. As he backed into the massive bulk of the New York Knickerbocker center, Willis Reed, the big Buck seemed to have four legs—two extra-long ones that reached to the floor of the basketball court, and the arms that appeared almost as long as they stretched far up toward the ceiling.

In the strong-fingered hands at the ends of those arms, a round leather ball was nestled—but it didn't stay there for more than a fraction of a second. As Reed leaned his muscular 240 pounds against Kareem, the Milwaukee center moved back a step. Reed, still leaning, had committed himself and Kareem was in full control. With the grace of a ballet-master, he rose on the toes of his left foot while his sinewy right arm made a wide arc that swept the ball far out of Reed's off-balance reach. Kareem's arm stopped at the peak of its swing, and a flick of the wrist sent the ball rolling off his fingertips. It curled away and, as the Knick pivotman optimistically wheeled toward the backboard for a possible rebound, the basketball skimmed the iron ring and slipped through the net.

Reed simply shrugged, a silent demonstration of his admiration and frustration. These two giants had been battling for years, and from the start Willis had been one of Kareem's strongest opponents and biggest admirers. After their first head-to-head battles in Kareem's rookie season (1969–70), Reed had said, "When I play against him, I know my game has to be at its very best. If he makes up his mind to score, it's practically impossible to stop him. It won't be long before he's head and shoulders above everybody else. No matter what happens, you don't think of stopping him. You just hope the other guys on his team don't hurt you too much. Right now there is nobody in the league who influences a game as much as he does. I admire anybody that tall with such body control, skill, coordination, and mobility. It's amazing that a guy his size can do what he does."

Kareem was big for his age from the day he was born on April 16, 1947, in New York City. His father was named Ferdinand Lewis Alcindor, and that was the name given to the baby that tipped the scales at 12 pounds, 11 ounces and measured $22\frac{1}{2}$ inches. It was the name he used until he chose in 1971 to be called Kareem Abdul-Jabbar after his conversion to the Islamic faith.

When Kareem's father was asked to describe his son's early years, Mr. Alcindor replied, "We were determined to bring Lewis up properly, as best we could, and give him respectable goals and guides in life. Of course, we are intensely proud of all his basketball accomplishments and of all the honors he has received, but we are just as proud that he got his education, his college degree.

"We are satisfied now that he is a decent person, sensitive and educated and aware, and we like to think that it would have turned out that way regardless of basketball. He had to be a man first, then an athlete."

As a child, Kareem was all that any parents could ask for. Intelligent and studious, he earned excellent grades in school. But he still found time for sports. Basketball was a natural part of his life, both because he was tall and because it was a "must-play" sport in the world of big-city kids. The tall, thin youngster also excelled in track, baseball, and football.

By the time he began high school at New York City's Power Memorial Academy, Kareem was by far the biggest—and the best—young hoopster in town. But Kareem had more going for him than his towering height. He also had remarkable coordination and agility. Throughout his career—in high school, college, and the NBA—opponents were astonished to see the lanky 7-footer weave his way along the boards, dribbling and shifting his body with the smoothness of a 6-foot guard.

"Lew is really something," said one Power Memorial teammate. "On one play he'd be in the pivot, taking a pass and whipping in one of those big hook shots. On the next time down, he'd get the ball about thirty feet from the hoop, fake his man, and go driving in for a lay-up. Only it wouldn't be a lay-up like a guard puts in. He'd go flying way up there and wham the ball down so hard, you expected to see the cords tear into threads. He's a guard, forward, and center all wrapped up in one big package."

Despite his explosive and exciting play, Kareem was never accused of being a grandstander. He did his job remarkably well but never seemed to seek the spotlight. In his quiet, efficient way, he poured in points, as serious about the game as he was about his studies. He had many hot streaks—games in which he scored anywhere from 30 to 50 points—but he always played with a facial expression that was less like a hot shot than an accountant working on income-tax reports—solemn and businesslike.

In Kareem's three-year varsity career, his team lost only one game. That was a 46-43 defeat to DeMatha High School, a contest that featured DeMatha's slow-down strategy designed to stifle Power Memorial's big gun at center.

Years later Power Memorial coach Jack Donohue recalled that game. "We won seventy-nine games with Lew at center, while losing only that one," he said. "But when we lost that game, Lew cried. He blamed himself for the defeat, moaned that he scored only sixteen points, and felt absolutely miserable. I tried to tell him that there would have been no way for us to have seventy-one in a row without him, that it was far from his fault, and so on. But it didn't help. I never saw a kid who hated to lose as much as Lew."

His competitive spirit and incredible basketball talent as a high-schooler soon brought Kareem to the nationwide attention of college and professional coaches, alike. Among them was Eddie Donovan, then coach of the New York Knickerbockers. When Kareem was still a junior at Power Memorial, Donovan declared, "Alcindor's the best high school player I've ever seen. He could step into my line-up right now."

He probably could have, but Kareem was in no

hurry to reach the pro ranks. First he wanted to obtain a college degree. Intent on learning as well as furthering his basketball career, Kareem chose to attend the University of California at Los Angeles (UCLA). And there, under the direction of coach John Wooden, he made basketball history. He spearheaded UCLA to three straight NCAA championships, was unanimously elected to three All-America teams, and was named Player of the Year twice. In earning those distinctions, the "Big A" scored a total of 2,325 points and collected 1,367 rebounds.

Scoring was far from his only contribution to UCLA, however. Consider the case for defense, Big-A style. Playing in his first varsity contest as a sophomore (freshmen weren't allowed to play varsity basketball), he shook up the University of Southern California squad with his all-around play. Naturally, he scored, contributing 56 points, to UCLA's 105–90 victory. But he also out-hustled and out-elbowed the tough USC big men to capture 21 rebounds. And that was done with two or three opponents banging him every chance they had. Even in that first game Kareem displayed his pro potential by getting rid of rebounds swiftly, snapping the ball downcourt to teammates to set up thrilling fast breaks and easy baskets.

To top it all off, he challenged the USC shooters with his demoralizing shot-blocking technique.

A jubilant Kareem Abdul-Jabbar (then known as Lew Alcindor) indicates UCLA's status after the Bruins won the NCAA championship.

That night he slapped away at least twelve shot attempts, a feat that often occurred in UCLA-dominated games throughout his college career. His opponents were awed and intimidated by the sight of the slender giant looming over them, creating an almost impassable barrier between the ball and the basket. As coach Wooden put it, "When Lew is on defense he cuts down the shooting percentage of the other team. They're afraid to shoot, and they are looking for him when they do shoot. So they don't shoot as well as they normally do."

Kareem's impact on college basketball was so forceful that the rulesmakers made a special change in an attempt to limit his scoring. Because he was so tall and had the ability to use his height so effectively, they legislated against dunking. It was obvious to everyone why the rule was changed, and it quickly became known throughout the country as "The Alcindor Rule."

If UCLA's rivals expected the new rule to neutralize Kareem, they were in for a big surprise. The dunk was by no means his only offensive weapon, and although Kareem didn't like the rule, he wasn't worried about his game. "I'll still get my points," he said.

And, of course, he did. Even without his dunk shot, Kareem was almost unstoppable. By the time he graduated with a degree in history, UCLA's basketball team had racked up a three-year history of 87 wins and just one loss. And that defeat had come against a Houston team that had edged UCLA, 71-69. Kareem played despite blurred vision caused by a minor eye injury which had kept him out of several games and practice sessions before the Houston match. Later that season, however, a healthy Kareem claimed revenge by leading UCLA to a 101-69 rout of that same Houston squad.

Wrapping up his three-year college career with a 26.4 points-per-game average, the gifted scorer-rebounder-blocker was a prize any professional team would have paid a fortune to sign. The lucky club turned out to be the Milwaukee Bucks, an expansion team that had made its NBA debut in 1968-69 and badly needed the big super-center. Milwaukee's first NBA season had ended with the Bucks last in their division with a 27-55 won-lost record. The Bucks gladly gave Kareem a $1,400,000 contract for his signature—and he was worth every penny of it.

In his first big-league season, the Big A was the uncontested Rookie of the Year. He earned that honor by scoring 2,361 points for an average of 28.8 a game, a mark topped only by scoring king Jerry West. And his 1,190 rebounds, averaging out to 14.5 a game, earned him third spot in the carom competition. With Kareem in the middle, the Bucks turned their 1968-69 record around and

Kareem shoots over another basketball giant—Wilt Chamberlain.

finished their second season with 56 wins and 26 losses to capture second place in their division.

"He's just too much," former All-Star guard and coach Bob Cousy said of Kareem. "A rookie and he's on the verge of dominating this league already —and he's just a kid!"

The "kid" came back for the 1970–71 campaign with a full pro season under his belt and a desire to top his freshman debut in every way possible. Just how well he did is reflected in the record posted by Milwaukee that year. The Bucks won 66 games against just 16 losses, then marched on to the NBA championship, blitzing the Bullets with four straight wins in the finals. In just two years, Kareem had brought a cellar-dwelling team to the very top. And in the process he had racked up a season's total of 2,596 points and a per-game mark of 31.7. Fittingly, Kareem Abdul-Jabbar won the NBA's Most Valuable Player award, finishing far ahead of his nearest competitor, Jerry West.

The 1971–72 season was another big one for Milwaukee's big man. Although the Bucks failed to repeat as league champions, it wasn't the fault of their peerless center. He captured the NBA's MVP title for the second year in a row, again far outdistancing runner-up Jerry West in the voting. Abdul-Jabbar's shot-blocking had become legendary, and the voters recognized the importance of that facet of basketball. But they were equally influenced by Kareem's rebounding at a rate of 16.6 a game and by his fantastic scoring. In the 1971–72 campaign the Big A-J shredded the nets for 2,822 points and a per-game average of 34.8. His blazing-hot shooting didn't merely lead the league, it was a full 6.6 points higher than the average of second-place scorer, Nate Archibald.

Every good big man is almost inevitably compared to the legendary Celtic center, Bill Russell. But in Kareem's case, it was Russell himself who made the comparison. Remarking about the brilliance of Kareem's hitting on hook shots, dunks, fade-away jumpers, and one-handed outside shots, Russell said, "He is a better shooter than I was. By far. He is more mobile, has better moves, a greater variety of shots, a nicer touch, and more places he can score from than any player of his size to come along. He can handle the ball and play defense."

Kareem enjoyed all the praise and the awards. But as proud as he was to be scoring champ and MVP, he was disappointed that the Bucks hadn't taken the league title again. "I can be very effective, sure," he said, "but my effectiveness isn't self-perpetuating unless it's used correctly. It becomes futile to keep passing the ball to me and expecting me to stuff it. Then the other team starts climbing all over me and I'm useless. I don't care whether I'm on your team or who's on your team, you've got to play as a team, got to do all your things and

Abdul-Jabbar goes up for his famous dunk shot while Golden State's Jeff Mullins watches helplessly from below.

mix 'em up to keep the opponent guessing. When all five guys are out there working, then the big guy's effective and stays effective."

The Bucks and their "big guy" continued to be effective in 1972–73 when they led the Midwest Division (although they again failed to recapture the NBA championship). This time Kareem finished second to Nate Archibald in the scoring race, ramming in 2,292 points at an average of 30.2 a game. His 16.1 rebounds a game were good for fourth place in the NBA.

At the end of the season Milwaukee coach Larry Costello said, "He is the greatest basketball player ever. He is extremely intelligent and easy to coach." But it was Abdul-Jabbar's ability—and willingness—to play a team game that pleased his coach most. "Sure, I know Kareem could score 100 points a game if he wanted to," Costello added. "But that's not what he's most interested in."

And when, in 1974, Kareem was asked about the possibility of his matching Wilt Chamberlain's record of 100 points in a game, the big Buck center answered, "Wilt did that in another era. I don't think it could be done now. If the chance were there for me to score 60 or 70 in a game, yes, I could do it . . . but only if I had to. You've got to keep everybody involved in the game. That is important if you want to win."

After facing Kareem in a 1974 contest the New

York Knicks' Jerry Lucas was exhausted by the effort of trying to stop the Bucks' pivotman. "Couldn't do it," the 6-foot-9 Lucas admitted. "He put in 38 points and grabbed I-don't-know-how-many rebounds. You don't know whether to front him, push him, or play him from the side. You know you can't stop him, and you know you can't surround him by yourself. All you can hope to do is curtail him.

"No doubt," Lucas continued, "that he's the best center who ever played the game. I know Wilt could get his points—but I mean Jabbar's ability, his shots, his moves, his quickness. He's the impossible man!"

Impossible because he dunked with his left hand or his right. Hooked with his left hand or his right. Dunked with two hands, facing the basket or over his head with his back to the hoop. Rebounded . . . screened for teammates . . . passed off for assists . . . blocked shots . . . intimidated every member of the opposing team . . . and scored, scored, scored!

Index

Page numbers in italics refer to photographs.

Abdul-Jabbar, Kareem, 53, 132–147
  college career, 138–141
  early life, 135–137
  photos of, *132, 139, 142, 145*
  with Milwaukee Bucks, 141–147
Alabama, University of, 33
Albeck, Stan, 12
Alcindor, Lew, 135
  see also Abdul-Jabbar, Kareem
Archibald, Nate, 144, 146
Atlanta Hawks, 35–41
Attles, Al, 69

Balter, Sam, 110
Baltimore Bullets, 57, 96, 143
  see also Capitol Bullets
Barry, Dennis, 60
Barry, Rick, 44, 56–71
  early life, 60–61

  photos of, *56, 63, 66, 70*
  with Golden State Warriors, 67–71
  with New York Nets, 65–67
  with Oakland Oaks, 64
  with San Francisco Warriors, 56–60, 61–64
  with Washington Capitols, 64–65
Baum, John, 103
Baylor, Elgin, 17, 61, 73
Bellamy, Walt, 35
Bianchi, Al, 17
Bing, Dave, 123
Boston Celtics, 89
Bradley, Bill, *80,* 87, 124
Bridges, Bill, 35
Brown, Larry, 101, 102
Brown, Roger, 101
Buffalo Braves, 129

Caldwell, Joe, 35
Capitol Bullets, 88
Carolina Cougars, 103
Carter, Fred, 131
Chamberlain, Wilt, 44, 53, 61, 103, 113, *115, 142,* 146
Chicago Bulls, 98
Chipley High School, 46
Cleamons, Jim, 96
Cleveland Cavaliers, 129
Costello, Larry, 146
Cousy, Bob, 33, 143
Cowens, Dave, 38, 126
Crawford, Fred, 123

Daniel High School, 27, 28
Daniels, Mel, 52, 101, 102, 112
DeBusschere, Dave, 58, 59, 68, 82, 89, 113
DeMatha High School, 137
Denver Rockets, 109–113
Detroit, University of, 109
Detroit Pistons, 123
Donohue, Jack, 137
Donovan, Eddie, 78, 79, 137

Edwards Military Academy, 27, 28
Elderkin, Phil, 117
Erving, Alexis, 12
Erving, Julius, 11–23, 53, 93, 100, 101
  early life, 12–16
  college career, 16
  photos of, *10, 15, 19, 22*
  with New York Nets, 20–23
  with Virginia Squires, 16–20
Erving, Marvin, 12

Frazier, Walt, 72–89

Gambee, Dave, 59
Gardner-Webb Junior College, 46
Gilmore, Artis, 17, 42–55
  college career, 46–49
  early life, 45–46
  photos of, *22, 42, 47, 51, 54*
  with Kentucky Colonels, 49–55
  with Golden State Warriors, 67–71
Golden State Warriors, 67–71
  see also San Francisco Warriors
Goodrich, Gail, 131
Gowdy, Curt, 49
Guerin, Richie, 35, 36, 38

Hannum, Alex, 59, 62
Hartman, Jack, 78
Havlicek, John, 62
Hawkins, Connie, 110
Hayes, Elvin, 69
Haywood, Spencer, 104–119, 131
  college career, 109
  early life, 105–108
  photos of, *104, 108, 111, 115, 118*
  with Denver Rockets, 109, 113
  with Seattle SuperSonics, 113–119
Hazzard, Walt, 35
Holzman, Red, 86
Houston, University of, 141
Houston Rockets, 39, 41
Howard High School, 77
Hudson, Lou, 35

Indiana Pacers, 50, 51, 52, 65, 92, 98–103
Indiana University, 92, 93, 95–98, 99
Issel, Dan, 17, 44, 65

Jacksonville University, 46–49
Johnson, Gus, 96, 113

INDEX 151

Johnson, Neal, 20
Jones, Wally, 123
Jukkola, Ralph, 33

Kenon, Larry, 53
Kentucky, University of, 95
Kentucky Colonels, 43, 44, 49–55
Knight, Bobby, 99

Ladner, Wendell, 53
Lanier, Bob, 113, 124
Leaks, Manny, 103
Leonard, Bob, 92, 102
Los Angeles Lakers, 70–71, 87
Los Angeles Stars, 110
Loughery, Kevin, 21, 23
Louisiana State University, 28–35, 38
Lucas, Jerry, 81, 147

Madison Square Garden, 76
Maravich, Pete, 24–41, 124, 126
 college career, 28–35
 early life, 26–28
 photos of, *24, 29, 32, 37, 40, 75*
 with Atlanta Hawks, 35–41
 with New Orleans Jazz, 41
Maravich, Press, 26, 27, 28, *29*, 31, 35
Massachusetts, University of, 16
McAdoo, Bob, 131
McDaniels, Jim, 96
McGinnis, George, 20, 21, 23, 50, 53, 90–103
 college career, 95–98
 early life, 93–95
 photos of, *90, 97, 102*
 with Indiana Pacers, 98–103
McKenzie, Stan, 122
McKinney, Bones, 45
Meely, Cliff, 96

Memorial Coliseum, 122
Mengelt, John, 96
Miami, University of, 57
Mieuli, Franklin, 59
Milwaukee Bucks, 132, 141–147
Moe, Doug, 18
Monroe, Earl, 38, 88
Mullins, Jeff, 68, *145*
Murphy, Calvin, 124

Needham-Broughton High School, 27
Netolicky, Bob, *66*
Newlin, Mike, 41
New Orleans Jazz, 41
New York Knicks, 68, 73, 76, 78, 79–89, 133–134, 137
New York Nets, 20, 44, 53, 55, 65–67
Nissalke, Tom, 119

Oakland Oaks, 64
Olsen, Bud, 51, 52

Paultz, Billy, 53, *54*
Pershing High School, 107
Petrie, Geoff, 38, 120–131
 early life, 124
 photos of, *120, 125, 128, 131*
 with Portland Trial Blazers, 124–131
Pettit, Bob, 28, 33
Philadelphia 76ers, 62, 123
Phoenix Suns, 98
Pittsburgh Condors, 65
Pittsburgh Ironmen, 26
Portland Trail Blazers, 121, 122, 124–131
Power Memorial High School, 126, 137
Princeton University, 124

Reed, Willis, 82, 87, 89, 133, 134
Robertson, Oscar, 34, *37*, 38, 95, 107
Russell, Bill, 44, 49, 53, 103, 110, 119, 144

San Diego Conquistadors, 11
San Francisco Warriors, 56–60, 61–64
  see also Golden State Warriors
Schulman, Sam, 114
Scott, Charlie, 67
Seattle SuperSonics, 105, 113–119, 121, 122
Selvy, Frank, 34
Sharman, Bill, 62, 114
Simon, Walt, 50
Snyder, Dick, 121, 122
Sojourner, Willie, 53
Southern Illinois University, 78–79

Tampa, University of, 33
Texas Chaparrals, 65
Thurmond, Nate, 44, 69, 70, 113
Todd, Rolland, 126, 127
Tresvant, John, 96
Trinidad Jr. College, 108

UCLA (University of California at Los Angeles), 48, 99, 138–141
USC (University of Southern California), 138
U.S. Olympic Team, 108–109
Unseld, Wes, 95, 96

Van Arsdale, Dick, 95, 128
Van Arsdale, Tom, 95
van Breda Kolff, Bill, 123
Virginia Squires, 11, 16–20

Walton, Bill, 99
Warley, Ben, 58
Washington Capitols, 64–65, 109
  see also Virginia Squires
Washington High School, 94
West, Jerry, 38, 116, 126, 127, 141, 143
Wicks, Sidney, 129, 130
Wilkens, Lennie, 82, 114, 122
Williams, Bernie, 12
Wooden, John, 138, 140

Youngstown Bears, 26